The Sunday Reset

The Sunday Reset

One Hour a Week to Feel Back in Control: A weekly routine to organise life without long planning sessions

Priya Dhanvel

Mindful Pages

Published in 2026

ISBN: 9789376558490 (PB)
ISBN: 9789376556007 (eBook)

Published by

Mindful Pages
Imprint of Alpha Editions LLC
312 W. 2nd St #1834
Casper, WY 82601, USA

This book was developed using advanced writing tools to support the drafting and ideation process. All content has been thoughtfully curated, refined, and reviewed to ensure quality and relevance.

Content

Introduction

In Houston, April 1970, the room was lit like a late-shift aquarium: dim consoles, green numerals, faces turned towards information rather than one another. A quiet fan-whirr sat beneath everything, and over it came that thin, familiar sound in every recording—the headset hiss. The headset hiss never stops. On 13 April, halfway to the Moon, Apollo 13 reported a bang and a shudder; the mission's language tightened into facts, checks, recalculations, the careful trimming away of anything that was not essential to getting three people back alive. What is striking, decades later, is not the drama of catastrophe but the discipline of attention. With oxygen bleeding away, there was no appetite for ambiguity. Loose ends became lethal. Every open question had to be either closed, parked with a name, or assigned to someone whose sole job was to carry it. Not because the engineers were more virtuous than the rest of us, but because uncertainty had a cost they could measure.

Most lives do not have Mission Control. Most lives do not even have a decent clipboard. Instead, they have a growing halo of half-decisions: an email kept unread because it contains a choice; a form put aside because it needs one missing number; a conversation postponed because it might be awkward; a household task that is "quick" only if one already knows where the batteries are. The days are not empty; they are crowded with micro-commitments and invisible obligations. The problem is rarely laziness. It is leakage. Attention leaks through small gaps, and the mind—built to notice unfinished things—keeps sending the same signals until something changes.

That background signal is not a melodrama. It is a low, steady pressure. A person can function perfectly well while carrying it, in the way one can work beside a dripping tap for weeks: the noise becomes part of the house, the drip becomes "normal", and yet the body registers it all the same. Many people are startled, when the drip finally stops, by how much quieter their internal world feels. They had not realised they were bracing. They had been paying, every day, for tasks they were not doing.

The modern week encourages this kind of bracing. Work is rarely finished; it is handed over, nudged along, revised, reopened. Domestic life has become a sophisticated logistics operation: childcare, deliveries, appointments, passwords, school messages, subscription renewals, parcels that need returning, packages that need collecting, repairs that require waiting at home for a window that is never exact. Even leisure is scheduled through apps that politely demand administration. Small obligations now arrive like raindrops rather than storms, which is precisely why they are hard to respect: each one is minor, but together they soak the coat. When the mind senses that it cannot quite account for what is coming, it improvises with stress. Stress is the brain's crude but effective way of saying, "Something is untracked."

A curious paradox follows. The more crowded the week becomes, the less time feels available to organise it, and yet the lack of organisation is what turns ordinary commitments into constant threat. It is not simply that disorganisation wastes minutes; it corrodes trust. Trust, here, is not a grand moral quality. It is the small, private confidence that if something matters it will be remembered, found, or handled at the right time. When that confidence weakens, the mind compensates by keeping everything close. It rehearses. It rechecks. It reopens the same mental file at inconvenient times—while brushing teeth, during a meeting, in bed. This is why the gentle instruction to "just write a list" so often fails; the issue is not the existence of a list, but whether the list is trusted enough to allow the mind to stop hovering. A system that is not trusted does not relieve pressure; it adds another place to worry.

A system becomes trusted through a blunt mechanism: repeated closure. Closure does not mean perfection. It means decisions are made and honoured. The crucial move is to take the week you have already lived—its surprises, its slipped promises, its overlooked details—and give it an ending that the brain recognises as real. There is a particular relief in naming what happened rather than letting it drift into the next set of days like fog. A missed appointment becomes either rescheduled or released. An unanswered message becomes replied to, delegated, or deleted. A task that keeps haunting becomes defined as a next action that can actually be done. The moment a thing is properly defined, it becomes smaller, even if the work itself is not small. Vagueness is the true weight. Precision is lighter.

Consider a familiar scene. It is late afternoon on a weekday. A person sits at a desk—work or kitchen table, the difference has blurred—and flicks between screens. There is a calendar with coloured blocks, a task app with dozens of items, a chat thread, a note with a half-formed plan, a browser with too many tabs. Each tool promises control, and yet each tool also demands attention: which version is true, where did that information go, what did I mean by that cryptic line, when did I last look at this? Tool sprawl looks like sophistication but behaves like friction. It produces duplication, contradictions, and a special kind of dread: the suspicion that somewhere, in one of the many places where information might live, there is something important being forgotten.

Governments and organisations have learned this at scale, because the cost of fragmentation becomes undeniable when it affects millions. When the UK Government Digital Service launched GOV.UK in October 2012 in London, part of its aim was brutally practical: consolidate sprawling information scattered across departmental websites into a single, coherent front door. The point was not aesthetic minimalism; it was reliability. If citizens could not find a form, or found the wrong version, the system generated needless calls, errors, delays. Duplication did not create choice; it created confusion. The lesson is not that a personal life should be run like a state platform. It is that reliability comes from reducing the number of places where the truth might be. When the truth has one home, the mind stops searching.

A weekly reset is a small, domestic version of that consolidation. It is a contained ritual with an unglamorous purpose: to restore a single source of truth for the week ahead, and to close enough loops from the week behind that attention stops spilling. The ritual matters because it is scheduled, not because it is sacred. Unscheduled organisation expands to fill any available space, which means it competes with rest, family, and whatever the week demands. Containment is the kindness. It prevents the strange fate of the conscientious person who "stays on top of things" by constantly thinking about them, like a juggler who never puts the balls down. The goal is not to become a juggler. The goal is to have a table.

One hour is not magic; it is a constraint. The constraint forces a particular quality of thought. Without a boundary, organisation turns into decorative rearrangement—rewriting lists, colour-coding, making the mess look tidy while leaving it essentially undefined. With a boundary, the mind is compelled to decide what can be closed quickly, what must be scheduled, what must be parked for a longer session, and what is noise dressed as obligation. That last category matters more than most people admit. Many open loops are not truly commitments; they are fantasies of who one might be if time were endless. Keeping them alive as "pending" drains energy while offering no return. A good weekly reset is not merely additive; it subtracts. It gives permission to stop carrying what does not fit.

Still, not every life yields gracefully to planning. Some weeks are governed by unpredictable care demands, shift patterns, acute crises, or the kind of work where emergencies are the job. In such weeks, organisation cannot promise calm. It can only promise fewer avoidable surprises. The difference is important. A weekly reset is not an attempt to control the world. It is an attempt to control what can be controlled: clarity about commitments, a realistic view of time, and a deliberate handover between weeks so that the mind is not forced to improvise under pressure. Even when the week is volatile, clarity has value. It prevents the extra suffering of guessing.

The arc of this approach is simple in principle and exacting in practice. First comes capture: drawing scattered thoughts, stray notes, screenshots, and mental reminders into a single inbox so they can stop living in the bloodstream. Capture is not reflection and not confession; it is logistics. Then comes review: a brief scan of what actually happened, what slipped, what needs follow-up, what surprised the schedule. A review is not a trial. It is a measurement. Then comes deciding: choosing what matters in the coming days, separating urgency from the theatre of urgency, turning vague intentions into next actions that can be completed in one sitting. Finally comes preparation: translating those decisions into a calendar that acknowledges hard commitments, buffers, and the reality that energy is uneven. Along the way, the reset touches the parts of life that produce the most friction—home basics, messages and paperwork, money awareness without the pretence of a full budgeting overhaul, relationships that suffer when connection is left to chance, and the physical and digital clutter that turns daily routines into obstacle courses. Each touchpoint is deliberately brief. The ambition is not to fix everything. The ambition is to stop the drip.

It helps to be honest about the nature of "small tasks". A two-minute job is rarely two minutes. It is two minutes plus the search for the right document, plus the decision about which option to choose, plus the follow-up reminder, plus the small social negotiation required to ask someone for something, plus the friction of switching contexts. The hidden cost of tiny tasks is set-up. When set-up is missing, tasks linger. They linger not because they are hard but because they are undefined. A person who writes "sort finances" is not postponing a task; they are postponing a dozen decisions. A person who writes "find last month's statement" has created a door handle: something the mind can grasp. Clear next actions are a form of respect for future time. They prevent avoidance from masquerading as busy-ness.

Calendar planning often fails for a similarly unromantic reason. Many plans are written as if time were smooth. Time is not smooth. Time has edges, and those edges cut. Travel takes longer than expected. A meeting overruns. A child gets sent home unwell. A train is delayed. The plan collapses not because the person is weak, but because the plan is brittle. Hard commitments placed without buffers become a chain of dominoes. A ten-minute gap, repeated, is the difference between a day that absorbs disruption and a day that shatters. When planning acknowledges friction—realistic travel, transition time, inevitable interruptions—it stops being an aspirational sketch and becomes a usable map. A usable map does not prevent detours, but it makes them less frightening.

There is also the question of energy, a factor that most productivity advice treats as an embarrassment. People plan as if the brain were available on demand: as if concentration were a tap one could turn on at 14:00 because the calendar says so. Concentration is a biological resource, not a moral virtue. It rises and falls with sleep, stress, nutrition, cycle, workload, emotional strain, and the simple accumulation of decisions. Planning that ignores energy turns into self-betrayal. Planning that honours it becomes, paradoxically, more ambitious, because it stops wasting the best hours on low-value tasks. Matching work to energy is not indulgence. It is efficiency with a human face.

The household, too, benefits from a certain kind of blunt realism. The aim is not a magazine home; it is a home that reduces weekday decision-making. A surface clear is not a declutter aesthetic; it is a reduction in search time and irritation. Laundry flow is not domestic virtue; it is the prevention of Monday morning chaos. Food basics are not culinary aspiration; they are fewer frantic purchases and fewer meals assembled from desperation. The cleverness of a fifteen-minute home reset is that it targets friction points rather than pursuing the fantasy of "catching up". Catching up is a myth. Maintaining function is achievable.

Money and administrative checks are handled with similar restraint. The intention is awareness: knowing what bills and obligations are approaching, noticing surprises early, and converting dread into specific actions. The alternative is the common pattern of avoidance until urgency arrives with teeth. Paperwork becomes frightening when it is unidentified. Messages become heavy when they are ambiguous. A short triage—do, defer, delegate, delete—does not solve every administrative problem, but it changes the emotional texture of the week. It prevents the mind from turning a pile of letters into a single, amorphous threat. It returns the work to its true size.

Relationships and wellbeing are woven into this not as sentimental garnish but as a recognition of where attention goes when the week is unmanaged. Emotional backlog accumulates in the same way administrative backlog does: unanswered conversations, worries that loop without resolution, small resentments that grow because there is no space to address them. Planned connection is not romantic; it is protective. A midweek call scheduled with intention can prevent a month of "we must catch up" guilt. A date to talk can turn a recurring anxiety into an appointment with reality. Sometimes the next step is as modest as a message. Modesty is allowed. The reset is not a stage.

Physical and digital clutter are also loops. A pile on the entryway table is a decision deferred: where does this belong, does it matter, will it leave the house? An overflowing downloads folder is the same decision, translated into pixels. A phone packed with duplicates is not merely untidy; it is a signal that attention has been taxed. Declutter practices that rely on heroic, occasional purges are brittle. The gentler method is to create a consistent exit route: a donate-and-discard lane that is always available, so that letting go is routine rather than dramatic. Again, the point is function. Beauty may appear as a side-effect. That is not the job.

Sustainability is the final discipline, and it is where many well-intentioned systems fail. The reset must bend with seasons: travel, illness, deadlines, family turbulence. A weekly ritual that works only in ideal conditions is a performance, not a tool. Consistency beats intensity. Missing a week is not moral failure; it is data. Recovery is part of the design. The most durable systems assume lapses and include a route back that does not involve self-punishment. The mind accepts what is repeatable. It resists what feels like a test.

The motif returns here, because it is not decorative. When the drip continues, people learn to live with it, and then they forget it is optional. When the drip stops, the silence is instructive: it reveals how much of life's stress is not caused by large tragedies but by small, persistent, unresolved things. The headset hiss of an unfinished week is similar. It is not always loud. It is constant. The relief is not in having no obligations. The relief is in knowing where they are, what they mean, and what will happen next.

A life that feels "back in control" is rarely a life with fewer responsibilities. It is usually a life with fewer unknowns. Control, in this sense, is clarity plus follow-through. Clarity without follow-through is merely another form of anxiety; follow-through without clarity is exhaustion. The weekly reset sits at the hinge between them. It asks for an hour, and in return it reduces the time spent rethinking the same problems. It converts a week from an improvisation into a considered sequence of decisions. It does not promise serenity. It promises fewer avoidable alarms.

The decision it invites is not dramatic. It is a trade-off between two kinds of effort: the effort of facing reality in a contained, deliberate session, or the effort of facing it repeatedly in fragments throughout the week. One kind of effort is chosen. The other is imposed. The diagnostic question, then, is simple enough to feel almost rude: where, exactly, is attention leaking—and what would change if the leak were named, closed, or parked with honesty?

Chapter 1
Why life admin piles up

A person is halfway through making tea when the phone buzzes. The message is ordinary, the sort that would be forgettable if it did not land on a small bruise of uncertainty: a reminder about an appointment that might be next week or might already have been missed, a note from school asking for a form that was meant to be returned, a delivery update that requires someone to be home at a particular time. The kettle clicks off with a blunt little finality. The mug warms the palm. The mind does not warm; it tightens. The message is not a crisis, and yet it has the flavour of one, because it arrives attached to a question the brain cannot answer quickly: what, exactly, is this asking of me?

The tea goes cold more often than people admit. Not because life is dramatic, but because attention is interrupted, re-routed, and held hostage by the unfinished. A person opens the email, reads just enough to feel the tug of responsibility, then closes it because there is no time to deal with it properly. A note is made, perhaps, but the note is vague. The question remains open, and the mind does what it is designed to do: it keeps the file in circulation. It resurfaces at inconvenient moments, not as a neat reminder but as a faint alarm. The day continues, outwardly normal, inwardly accompanied by a low-level sense of something pending.

This is how life admin begins to feel like a swarm. Not because the tasks are inherently difficult, but because they are incomplete in a particular way: they have not been turned into decisions. There is a difference between knowing that something exists and knowing what you are going to do about it. The first is information; the second is closure. Many people live with an impressive tolerance for the first and an exhausted relationship with the second. The result is a kind of background static that comes and goes, never loud enough to force a dramatic intervention, always present enough to steal ease.

The central tension is deceptively simple. The mind wants certainty and clean edges; life produces half-requests, partial information, and obligations that arrive mid-stride. When we do not have time to settle those edges, we carry them. Carrying feels responsible in the moment, but it quietly multiplies the work: every half-finished item demands periodic re-reading, re-remembering, re-deciding. The trade-off is not between being organised and being spontaneous. It is between choosing when to face ambiguity or allowing ambiguity to choose for you, again and again, in fragments.

That matters because attention is not merely a mental preference. It is a finite resource that determines the quality of everything else: the quality of work, the tone of conversations, the patience available for family, the capacity to rest without feeling watched by one's own to-do list. When attention is continually snagged by unresolved details, the week becomes a sequence of interruptions rather than a sequence of intentions. People become reactive without noticing the shift. They start to treat the urgent-looking as urgent, because it is the only thing their nervous system can reliably identify, and they begin to distrust quieter priorities simply because they do not shout.

It also matters because many of these obligations are not isolated. They are linked systems. One delayed email can trigger a missed appointment, which triggers a rescheduling call, which triggers time off work, which triggers childcare rearrangements, which triggers another set of messages. The original task was small. The ripples are not. Life admin piles up when small things remain in the wrong state: not finished, not deleted, not assigned, not scheduled, not transformed into a clear next move. A backlog is less about volume than about the number of items that still require thinking.

The surprising part is that what feels like busyness is often undecidedness. A person can spend an entire week "dealing with things" and still feel behind, because the work they did was not the work that closes loops. They scanned, they skimmed, they postponed, they left themselves notes that required further interpretation. They did not fail through lack of effort; they failed through poor definition. A tiny task with missing information is not a tiny task. It is a question waiting to be answered, and unanswered questions are sticky. They adhere to the mind, they reattach themselves after interruptions, they generate a sense of urgency without providing a way out.

And yet there is a trap on the other side. When people notice this stickiness, they often reach for an ideal of total control: the perfectly ordered life, the immaculate list, the week planned without gaps. That ideal is seductive because it promises peace, but it also converts organisation into performance. It creates a standard that cannot survive ordinary human days. The moment the plan is disrupted, the mind swings from "I am in control" to "I have lost control", and the very system meant to reduce stress becomes another arena for self-criticism. The more severe the standard, the more fragile the control.

The path here begins with noticing the nature of the ping: why unfinished things return and why they masquerade as urgency, even when they are merely unresolved. It then moves into the hidden machinery inside small tasks, the decisions and set-up work that make them linger far beyond their apparent size. It finally lands on a more durable kind of control, one that is satisfied by being *clear enough to move on* rather than being perfect enough to impress an imaginary auditor. Each step is less about effort and more about precision: the difference between vague obligation and a concrete next action, between an open loop and a settled one.

If life admin feels like it is always multiplying, the question is not how to work harder at it. The question is where the mind is being asked to hold uncertainty it cannot safely store. What is the one unfinished thing that keeps resurfacing, not because it is important, but because it is undefined?

Open loops and attention

In Berlin in 1927, the psychologist Bluma Zeigarnik published an observation that has refused to stay politely inside the laboratory. People, she reported, tended to remember interrupted tasks better than completed ones (Zeigarnik, 1927). The claim has been repeated so often it risks sounding like folklore, but its staying power points to something ordinary and stubborn: the mind treats the unfinished as unfinished, even when the body has moved on. In a cafe, a waiter who has not yet closed the bill keeps the order in mind; once paid, it fades. In an office, an email read but not decided lingers with similar persistence. The modern version is quieter than a cafe and more relentless. The screen goes dark. The thought remains. Unfinished tasks keep calling back. A small, invisible ping.

Picture a familiar Monday. A calendar is open, the day is blocked, the laptop is awake, and yet the mind is already splitting into side-threads. One thread is the meeting starting in twenty minutes. Another is the message that arrived last night about rescheduling an appointment. Another is the form that needs "one last detail", which turns out to be three. Nothing here is dramatic. That is the point. The stress is not produced by a single emergency but by a flock of near-emergencies, each one asking to be held "for now". Attention becomes a kind of unpaid courier service, carrying parcels that no one has signed for.

The first thing to understand is that this is not a character flaw. The persistence of open loops has an architecture. The brain is an organ that predicts and resolves. It likes things it can count as complete because completion allows it to stop monitoring. When a task remains unresolved, the monitoring continues, and monitoring has a subjective feel: a background hum, a recurring thought, a twitch of irritation at the wrong moment. The idea that unfinished tasks intrude has been examined with more precision than the popular retelling suggests. In a set of experiments, Masicampo and Baumeister reported that unfulfilled goals increased intrusive thoughts and that forming a concrete plan reduced those intrusions (Masicampo and Baumeister, 2011). The implication is sharp. What troubles attention is not merely "having a lot to do". It is *not knowing what will happen next* with what needs doing. Uncertainty is sticky.

This stickiness creates a counterfeit form of urgency. An open loop does not only remind; it *presses*. It produces a sensation that resembles importance, because the mind is treating the unresolved item as a live variable. A person receives an unread email about an appointment. Until it is opened and decided, the mind cannot place it. Is it tomorrow? Is it a cancellation? Is it a problem? The brain does not like unknowns with potential consequences, so it keeps the item warm. This can look, from the inside, like responsible vigilance. It is often just ambiguity management. The behaviour is easy to spot in the body: glancing at the inbox again, reopening the calendar, rereading the same message. Time is spent, but nothing progresses. The ping persists.

The cognitive mechanism here is not mystical; it is a trade between storage and action. Working memory is limited. It is meant for immediate reasoning, not long-term warehousing of obligations. Yet an open loop demands repeated checking precisely because it has not been converted into a stable external commitment. The mind keeps it in circulation to prevent loss. This is why people who are outwardly competent can feel inwardly scattered: their competence has recruited their attention as the safety net. They remember because they are vigilant. Vigilance has a cost. It drains the very attention that would make the actual work easier.

A second, subtler mechanism follows. Open loops do not simply occupy mental space; they distort perception. When a task is undefined, the brain fills in the blanks with threat. The task becomes larger in imagination than it is in reality. "Sort the insurance" is not one thing; it is a cloud of potential complications. The mind, unable to see the boundary, treats it as a risk. Risk, in human cognition, triggers monitoring. Monitoring feels like urgency. Urgency demands attention. Attention is stolen from the present. The loop tightens. Notice how concrete verbs break the spell. "Find the policy number" is not a cloud. It is a handle. The point is not that every life task can be reduced to one simple move, but that attention calms when it can *measure* the next step.

The claim that unfinished tasks pull attention is not restricted to personal organisation; it shows up wherever stakes make ambiguity intolerable. In Houston in April 1970, Mission Control treated unresolved issues as operational hazards. During Apollo 13, engineers famously worked with checklists and disciplined decision trails, narrowing possibilities and closing questions because open questions were dangerous in a system with limited oxygen and limited time. The scene is not invoked to romanticise crisis. It is invoked because it exposes a principle in a clean, exaggerated form: when consequences are high, humans do not rely on "keeping it in mind". They externalise, assign, decide, and close. They reduce open loops because open loops absorb cognition. The implication for ordinary life is not to behave like a flight controller, but to recognise how much hidden effort is spent simulating control inside the head.

A more domestic, equally checkable example sits on the other end of the drama spectrum: the development of a single government website to replace hundreds of scattered ones. GOV.UK launched in October 2012 in the UK, consolidating public information and services under one domain. The design ethos was not decorative. Fragmentation creates rework: citizens search, fail, call; staff repeat explanations; outdated pages persist; forms get missed. Centralisation reduces the number of places where the truth might be. This is a structural solution to an attention problem at scale. The personal analogue is plain. When commitments and reminders live in too many locations, attention becomes the search engine. It keeps querying the system because the system is inconsistent. Reliability reduces the need for monitoring. Monitoring is what open loops provoke.

If open loops are so cognitively expensive, why do intelligent people tolerate them? Because a loop can feel like progress. Reading an email without deciding anything still creates the sensation of "handling" it. Making a vague note still creates the sensation of "capturing" it. Moving a form from one pile to another still creates the sensation of "organising". The body did something. The mind remains unconvinced. A helpful distinction emerges here between motion and commitment. Motion is visible. Commitment is decisive. Attention cares about commitment. It does not care that a task was seen; it cares that the task has a known fate. Will it be done at a certain time? Delegated to someone? Deleted because it no longer matters? Parked with a named next step? Until the fate is clear, the ping continues.

This is where "real urgency" and "mental noise" begin to separate. Real urgency is tethered to an external constraint: a deadline, a fixed appointment, a dependency that blocks others, a cost that changes with time. It shows up in calendars, confirmations, delivery windows, due dates, travel times, and promises made to actual humans who will be affected. Mental noise mimics urgency but floats free of constraint. It is the repeated thought without a deadline, the worry without a next action, the task that feels pressing because it is uncomfortable rather than time-sensitive. The difference is not moral. It is diagnostic. One can *check* real urgency against the world; mental noise keeps forcing internal rehearsal because the world has not been consulted or cannot yet be resolved.

A useful way to see this is to watch how the mind behaves around each type. With real urgency, attention tends to narrow. It asks practical questions: what is due, when, what must happen beforehand, what will fail if this is missed? With mental noise, attention tends to scatter. It generates more thoughts rather than more facts. It revisits the same item, seeking relief through rumination. The metric is not mood but outcome. After thinking about a truly urgent item for five minutes, there is usually a changed external state: a meeting booked, a message sent, a document found, a decision logged. After thinking about mental noise for five minutes, there is often only a tired brain and the same unresolved item, now with extra emotional residue.

There is an important limitation to acknowledge, because the "open loops are bad" story is too neat to be entirely true. Some forms of incompletion are useful. Creative work often requires leaving problems partially open so the mind can incubate, notice patterns, and return with a better idea. Research on mind-wandering and incubation suggests that stepping away from a problem can sometimes improve insight, particularly for tasks that benefit from broad associative thinking (for a classic discussion, see Sio and Ormerod, 2009, a meta-analysis on incubation effects). The point is not that leaving things unfinished is always harmful. The point is that different kinds of unfinishedness behave differently. A half-written paragraph can be productive incompletion because it is tethered to a chosen project and returns at an appropriate moment. An unpaid bill that is "somewhere" is corrosive incompletion because it returns as a threat, not as a creative prompt. One kind is held open deliberately. The other is left open by default.

Reconciling this limitation clarifies the deeper principle: attention is not allergic to incompletion; it is allergic to *unmanaged* incompletion. The mind can tolerate an open loop when it trusts that the loop has a container. In creative work, the container is often a project boundary, a document, a studio practice, a shared understanding that the work is in progress.

In life admin, the container is too often the skull. The container is vigilance. Vigilance is an unstable container because it competes with everything else and collapses under fatigue. When the container is external and reliable, the mind can let go without losing track. When the container is internal and fragile, the mind compensates by pinging more often. The ping is not the problem. It is the symptom.

The quiet motif returns: the ping is information, not judgement. When a thought keeps resurfacing, it is rarely saying, "You are failing." It is more often saying, "This has no safe place to live." Treating the ping as a signal changes its meaning. It becomes less like a scolding and more like an alarm from a smoke detector that cannot tell whether the kitchen fire is real or just burnt toast. The alarm's job is not to be polite; it is to be noticed. The human job is to determine whether the alarm corresponds to an external constraint or an internal itch, and then to decide what state change would allow the alarm to stand down.

A final complication: open loops do not simply come from tasks. They come from commitments that are social and ambiguous. A strained conversation postponed. A message drafted but unsent because it might upset someone. A decision deferred because it involves trade-offs that cannot be resolved in one sitting. These are not mere "admin" in the narrow sense, and yet they behave like admin in attention. They loop because the mind cannot file them. They feel urgent because they are unresolved. They steal attention because they carry emotional charge. The behaviour that reveals their nature is familiar: replaying the conversation in the shower, rehearsing what to say, checking for replies, interpreting silence. Even here, the distinction between real urgency and mental noise still applies. Sometimes there is a concrete next event that demands preparation. Often there is only the discomfort of leaving something unsettled.

This is why life admin piles up even in a life that looks, from the outside, successful. Professional competence often increases the number of commitments others place on a person and increases the range of systems they must interact with. It also makes them adept at coping. Coping is a brilliant short-term skill. It is a poor long-term strategy when it requires continuous attention. The more capable the person, the more they become the default safety net for their own life: they remember, they patch, they improvise. Improvisation works until it does not. Eventually, the mind begins to treat everything as potentially urgent, because it has learned that even small oversights can cascade. That learning is not irrational. It is simply exhausting.

The forward tension, then, is not whether to be organised. It is whether to keep paying the attention tax. Every open loop is a small loan taken against future calm: a promise that the mind will remember, return, and resolve later. Sometimes that loan is worth it. Sometimes it funds creative incubation or a deliberate pause. Often it is taken without consent, simply because the next action is unclear. The diagnostic test is quietly uncomfortable: when the ping arrives, is it pointing to a real external constraint that can be checked, or to a piece of ambiguity that has been allowed to live as a feeling rather than a decision?

The hidden cost of tiny tasks

On 30 October 1935 at Wright Field in Dayton, Ohio, the Boeing Model 299 lifted off and then faltered, stalling and crashing in front of onlookers. The aircraft itself was not the problem; it was a new kind of complexity. Investigators attributed the accident to a missed step: the gust locks were still engaged. Aviation lore remembers this moment as an origin story for the checklist, not because pilots suddenly became more diligent, but because a single overlooked detail could defeat experience. A small thing. A large consequence. The lesson is unnervingly portable: what looks like a minor action can contain hidden prerequisites, and when those prerequisites are missing, the action stops being minor.

Tiny tasks breed in the seams of everyday life because they arrive with a misleading label. "Just reply." "Just book it." "Just send the form." Language minimises. Reality does not. The mind reads the label and assumes the task will slip neatly into a gap between meetings or between dinner and sleep. Then the task opens like a set of nesting boxes: the information is not to hand, the password has expired, the right document cannot be found, the decision is not actually simple, the follow-up requires another person who is not available. Friction appears. Time leaks. The task remains unfinished, now heavier for having been opened and abandoned.

Small tasks rarely stay small.

The difficulty is not that the work is hard in any heroic sense. The difficulty is that small tasks are often *systems* masquerading as actions. Consider the everyday job of "booking an appointment". The visible action is a click or a call. The hidden work is the choice of date, the search for availability, the check against other commitments, the travel time, the confirmation, the reminder, the cancellation policy, the rescheduling if something changes. The task lingers because the brain senses the hidden steps and refuses to pretend they do not exist. What looks like procrastination is frequently an accurate objection: this is not a single action, so it cannot be treated as one. The implication is practical and slightly humiliating. Many "two-minute jobs" are not short; they are undefined.

This is why "little things" accumulate into a backlog that feels strangely oppressive. Each tiny item carries a cognitive toll before it even begins. There is the time spent remembering it exists, the time spent locating what it depends on, the time spent switching into the right context, and the time spent cleaning up after the interruption. Research on task switching has repeatedly shown that shifting attention between tasks imposes measurable costs in speed and accuracy, even when people believe they are multitasking efficiently (Rubinstein, Meyer, and Evans, 2001). The point is not to worship productivity research. It is to name what is happening in lived experience: a supposedly minor job becomes a detour because it drags the mind across boundaries. The detour is the hidden cost.

A simple scene exposes the mechanics. A person sits down to send a quick message confirming a meeting. They open the inbox. They cannot find the thread because it is buried under newsletters and automated updates. They search, skim, and get distracted by another email that seems urgent because it has a subject line in capitals. They click it, read half, and feel a pulse of responsibility. They close it. They return to the original message and realise they do not know the meeting location. They open the calendar. The calendar entry is vague. They search for the previous notes. The notes are in a different app. The app is full of half-ideas. Ten minutes pass. The message is still not sent. The mind now holds two open loops instead of one: the meeting confirmation and the newly discovered urgent-looking email. Nothing dramatic occurred. The system simply revealed its gaps. The implication is brutal: tiny tasks generate more work when they expose missing information.

The human brain treats missing information like a risk signal. Risk is not an abstract category; it changes behaviour. It makes people check again, keep the tab open, leave the email unread as a crude form of "do not forget". The behaviour is visible: repeated glances, reopened apps, the same thought resurfacing at inconvenient times. The risk is not always real, but the brain cannot assume that, because the cost of being wrong can be high. A missed appointment, a late fee, an awkward professional delay, a broken promise to someone who matters. The mind responds as it was built to respond: it monitors uncertainty. Monitoring feels like effort. Effort feels like urgency. The task grows in emotional weight, even if its objective difficulty is unchanged.

Here the motif matters: the checkbox. A tiny task often fails not because the checkbox is hard to tick, but because the box is not actually defined. People carry a vague mental checkbox that reads "deal with that", and the vagueness is the trap. It invites repeated partial engagement: opening, scanning, postponing, hoping the right moment will magically appear. The checkbox remains unticked, and because it remains unticked, it continues to demand attention. Defining the box changes the mind's relationship to it. The mind can tolerate a clear, bounded incompletion. It struggles with a foggy one. A foggy checkbox becomes a permanent notification.

A second named example shows how a "small detail" can become an organisational catastrophe when systems assume the detail will be handled somewhere, by someone, without being explicitly owned. On 23 September 1999, NASA lost the Mars Climate Orbiter when a mismatch in measurement units between teams contributed to navigation errors. The story is often told as a punchline about metric versus imperial, but it is better understood as a parable about invisible hand-offs. A tiny conversion, left implicit, became a failure at scale. The implication is not that everyday life is aerospace engineering. It is that tiny tasks become dangerous when they sit between systems, between people, between assumptions. Anything that depends on "someone will sort it" is an open loop with a professional accent.

The hidden cost of tiny tasks also explains a particular kind of shame: the shame of being delayed by something "stupid". People berate themselves for not renewing a simple subscription, not returning a basic form, not sending a short email. They assume the problem is laziness or lack of discipline. Often the problem is that the task has been misclassified. It is not "renew subscription". It is "find the login details", "decide whether this is still needed", "check the payment card", "compare the alternatives", "cancel the trial that is linked to it", "ensure the receipt goes to the right place". Each sub-step may be quick, but the chain is long, and chains snap at the weakest link: missing information, unclear criteria, a dependency on another person's response. Misclassification produces predictable failure. The mind resists starting because it knows, from experience, that the task will not finish cleanly.

This is where the idea of treating tiny tasks as mini-projects becomes less like a managerial indulgence and more like intellectual honesty. A mini-project is not a grand plan. It is a recognition that some actions require set-up, a decision, and a follow-up, and that bundling those elements into one vague item is a recipe for repeated interruption. The distinctive feature of a mini-project is that it needs a clear next move that is not the whole thing. The next move is a state change: a missing number located, a file retrieved, a question asked of the relevant person, a decision criterion chosen, a time reserved for the longer work. Notice how this changes the metric. Instead of measuring success as "task completed", it measures success as "task made runnable". Runnable tasks do not haunt attention in the same way, because they no longer depend on improvisation.

A limitation deserves respect here. Not every tiny task should be expanded into a project, and not every life benefits from increased granularity. Excessive decomposition can become its own form of avoidance, a way of producing the sensation of control while delaying action. Some people, especially those who find comfort in systems, can create so much scaffolding that the scaffolding becomes the work. The checkbox multiplies. The day disappears into organisation. This is not a moral failing either; it is a common response to anxiety. The reconciliation is to keep the purpose in view: definition exists to reduce repeated thinking, not to create a second job. When a task is truly trivial and truly self-contained, its best form may be immediate completion, not analysis. The skill is not to treat everything as a project, but to spot the items whose hidden steps will otherwise keep generating detours.

The difference can be observed in behaviour. A genuinely tiny task tends to be done in one uninterrupted burst: open, complete, close. A mislabelled tiny task tends to be opened and abandoned, repeatedly. It creates residue: tabs left open, drafts saved, reminders scribbled, a lingering sense of "I should". Residue is a diagnostic signal. It suggests the task has dependencies that have not been named, or decisions that have not been made, or context that is not available in the moment. The residue is evidence. It is also a cost. It consumes attention every time it is seen. It creates a low-level sense of being behind, even when much has been done.

Seen through this lens, "efficiency" stops being a macho pursuit of speed and becomes a gentler pursuit of fewer detours. "Trust" stops being a personality trait and becomes a system property: the confidence that when a task is noted, it is noted in a form that can be acted on without re-interpreting it. "Risk" stops being a distant business term and becomes the concrete dread of surprise bills, missed deadlines, awkward apologies, and the small reputational damage of being the person who "meant to" but did not. Each abstraction earns its place only when it points to a behaviour: fewer re-checks, fewer reopened messages, fewer stranded drafts, fewer late-night mental rehearsals.

The checkbox motif returns because it is so ordinary. People think the problem is the number of boxes. Often the problem is that too many boxes contain fog. Foggy boxes invite repeated engagement without closure, and repeated engagement is what makes life admin feel endless. The task does not go away when it is postponed; it becomes a background process, consuming attention in tiny bursts. That is the hidden cost. It is paid in minutes and in mood. It is paid in the quality of other work. It is paid in the inability to rest without interruption.

The forward test is uncomfortable precisely because it is specific. When a supposedly small task has been avoided for days, what is it really made of: missing information, an unmade decision, a dependency, or a fear of what it might uncover? The answer determines whether the next step is genuinely tiny or whether the tiny label has been a polite lie.

Control without perfection

On 15 January 2009, US Airways Flight 1549 struck birds shortly after take-off and lost thrust in both engines. Captain Chesley Sullenberger and First Officer Jeffrey Skiles brought the aircraft down on the Hudson River in New York City with all 155 people surviving. The public memory often clings to the cinematic image of a plane floating between ferries and winter light, but inside the cockpit the moment was made of something less glamorous: constrained decisions, prioritised actions, and a relentless refusal to chase the impossible. There was no time for a perfect plan. There was time for the next right move. The checklist mattered because it narrowed attention to what counted. No heroics. Just judgement.

Perfection is a strange seduction. It looks like control from a distance, tidy and complete, but it behaves like a trap when applied to the mundane machinery of life admin. Perfection demands total closure, total order, total foresight. Life does not comply. Calendars shift. People cancel. Children get ill. Trains run late. A person starts to treat organisation as a performance, an attempt to build a flawless week that will never be interrupted, and the moment interruption arrives the entire structure feels compromised. A small slip begins to register as failure rather than variance. The mind tightens. The work multiplies.

Good enough is powerful.

The shift from perfection to control begins with a more honest definition of what control is. Control is not the absence of loose ends; it is the reduction of attention leakage. It is the ability to stop thinking about the same unresolved item in five different moments of the day because its status is stable: decided, scheduled, delegated, deleted, or parked with a clear next move. That stability is an engineering problem more than a moral one. The mind wants to know whether it must keep monitoring. When a task is ambiguous, monitoring continues. When it is clear, monitoring can stop. The practical standard is not "everything finished". It is *clear enough to move on*. The implication is subtle but profound: organisation that does not reduce mental monitoring is decorative.

This matters because perfectionism has a recognised psychological shape, and it does not reliably produce better outcomes. Researchers have long distinguished between striving for high standards and the more punishing habit of equating mistakes with personal failure. The latter cluster is often what people mean by perfectionism in everyday life, and it tends to be linked with rumination, overchecking, and avoidance (Frost et al., 1990; Hewitt and Flett, 1991). Those behaviours have a tell: they create movement without closure. A person rewrites a list instead of deciding what belongs on it. They revisit an inbox instead of ending the open loops inside it. They add categories and colours until the system feels impressive, and then feel oddly less able to act because the system has become another thing to maintain. The metric is visible. The number of re-checks rises. The number of completed commitments does not.

A scene from ordinary work shows how perfectionism borrows the costume of responsibility. Someone is preparing a short email to confirm a meeting time. They draft. They edit. They add context "just in case". They reread. They worry that the tone is wrong. They consider whether to propose alternatives. The email remains unsent, not because the task is complex, but because the standard has quietly shifted from "confirm time" to "compose an impeccable message that cannot be misread". The cost is not only the delay. The cost is the attention held hostage by an unfinished, low-stakes item. The mind keeps it warm. It pings. Meanwhile, the meeting itself is no longer the only variable; the person's sense of competence is now at stake. A tiny task has become a referendum.

The central concept underneath this is older than productivity culture and more exacting than it. Herbert Simon used the term "satisficing" to describe decision-making that aims for an adequate solution rather than an optimal one, especially under constraints of time and information (Simon, 1956). That word matters because it gives dignity to an unglamorous truth: optimality is often unattainable, and chasing it can degrade results by consuming resources better spent elsewhere. In life admin, the resource is attention. The behaviour that signals satisficing is not carelessness; it is commitment to a decision threshold. An appointment is scheduled with sufficient information, not every possible detail. A task is broken into a next action that makes progress, not an entire project plan. A message is sent with clarity, not perfection. The implication is that control can increase while perfection decreases, because the mind stops monitoring what has been settled.

A second checkable anchor helps because it shows that "good enough" is not a personal coping strategy; it is a design principle in systems that must function. When GOV.UK launched in October 2012 in the United Kingdom, part of its design philosophy was ruthless simplification: fewer pages, fewer duplicate routes to the same service, fewer opportunities for a citizen to end up in the wrong place. The aim was not to display the full complexity of government but to make the essential path reliable. That choice embodies a form of satisficing at scale. A system can either try to represent everything perfectly, which often produces a maze, or it can commit to what a user needs to do next, clearly, without needless branching. The personal parallel is uncomfortable. Many people try to build a perfect representation of their lives in their tools. They would do better to build a reliable path through it.

The hardest part of adopting "clear enough" is not intellectual. It is emotional. Perfection feels like safety, especially for high-functioning people whose lives have rewarded conscientiousness. A flawless list looks like a promise that nothing will be missed. But that promise is counterfeit. Life produces new inputs faster than any list can be perfected, and the attempt to keep up creates a second stream of work: maintaining the appearance of control. The mind can become more loyal to the system than to reality. When that happens, stress increases even as organisation increases, because the person is now managing two things: their commitments and their standard. The standard becomes a silent supervisor, always dissatisfied.

There is, however, a credible limitation that deserves to be spoken plainly. Some domains cannot accept "good enough" in the casual sense. Aviation, surgery, nuclear operations, and certain forms of laboratory work carry risks where small errors can be catastrophic. In such contexts, perfection is not an aesthetic preference but a safety requirement. The reconciliation is important: the answer is not to import perfectionism into everyday life, but to notice how high-stakes domains actually achieve reliability. They do it by reducing reliance on memory and mood. They use checklists, redundancy, cross-checks, and clear handovers. They build systems that allow humans to be human without making human fallibility fatal. The lesson for life admin is not to raise the standard until it hurts. The lesson is to externalise the right details so the mind does not have to monitor everything. Even in high-stakes work, the goal is not a perfect human. It is a trustworthy process.

This is where "background stress" becomes a more meaningful measure than an empty task list. An empty list can be a fantasy, achieved by omitting what is uncomfortable or by pushing items into a vague "someday" fog. It can also be achieved by spending half a day reorganising rather than acting. Background stress, by contrast, has behavioural signatures. Fewer late-night mental rehearsals. Fewer compulsive inbox checks. Fewer moments of sudden panic because something "must have been forgotten". Fewer sticky notes with cryptic reminders that require re-interpretation. More clean endings to small actions: open, decide, close. These are not moral victories. They are reductions in monitoring load. They indicate that attention is being reclaimed.

The quiet motif here is the tick mark, not as a fetish of completion but as a signal that a decision threshold has been met. A tick is not a trophy; it is a permission slip. It tells the mind, "Stop carrying this." When people chase perfection, they delay the tick because the item must be finished in the most ideal way. When people chase control, they earn the tick by making the item stable: by turning uncertainty into a committed next step, even if the entire project remains incomplete. The tick, in this sense, is not about accomplishment. It is about containment. It is the difference between a task that lives in the brain and a task that lives in a system.

The forward tension is not whether perfection is admirable. It often is. The tension is whether perfection is being deployed where it helps, or where it simply converts ordinary life into a constant audit. The diagnostic question is sharp enough to sting: when an item lingers for days as "small but undone", is the real obstacle effort, or is it the hidden demand that it be settled flawlessly rather than *clear enough to move on*?

Chapter 2
Designing your Sunday Reset hour

The hour begins with good intentions and ends in fragments. A person sits down on a Sunday with a cup of tea, opens a laptop, tells themselves they will get organised, and immediately discovers three competing realities: the house is louder than expected, the week ahead is already crowded, and their information is scattered across places that do not agree with one another. A calendar here, a note there, messages that feel too important to ignore, tasks written in several styles for several moods. They start by tidying the list, then jump to an email, then chase a document, then remember a household errand, then notice the laundry. The kettle clicks again. The tea cools. The hour dissolves into motion without the clean relief of closure.

Another Sunday looks different but fails for the same underlying reason. The person protects the time, sits at a desk, puts on headphones, and tries to be serious about it. They open a new app because the old one feels messy. They migrate tasks. They adjust labels. They create a colour system. They scroll, edit, polish. It feels industrious. It is also strangely hollow, because the mind keeps asking the same question it asked in the previous chapter: what is the status of the things that actually matter? When the hour ends, the week is no clearer than before, only better decorated. The mind remains on call.

The tension is not a lack of discipline. It is the clash between a ritual that must be small and a life that refuses to be neatly contained. If the reset becomes negotiable, it disappears. If it becomes too large, it becomes resented. If it becomes too vague, it becomes a performance. The trade-off is exacting: an hour that is protected must also be bounded; an hour that is bounded must have a reliable shape; a reliable shape requires decisions about where the truth lives, how it is processed, and how the session ends. The aim is not to make the hour impressive. The aim is to make it dependable, even when the week has been untidy.

Design matters because willpower is a poor long-term strategy for anything that must recur. People often treat planning as a cognitive act, a matter of thinking harder, yet the more durable changes come from shaping the environment and the sequence so that less thinking is required at the point of execution. A consistent slot reduces internal bargaining. A consistent place reduces friction. A minimal toolset reduces the draining question of which system is authoritative. When those choices are settled, attention can be used for decisions rather than for managing the act of organising itself. The hour stops competing with the rest of life and starts behaving like a quiet maintenance routine.

The stakes are not abstract. A weekly reset that works changes what a person does on an ordinary Tuesday afternoon. It reduces the number of times they reopen the same messages. It reduces the small panics caused by half-remembered obligations. It reduces the late-night rehearsal of tomorrow. That is not a sentimental benefit. It is a measurable behavioural shift: fewer checks, fewer searches, fewer improvised rescues. It also affects relationships and work quality in the simplest possible way. When the mind is not busy guarding loose ends, it listens better. It finishes more cleanly. It rests without being constantly pulled back to a mental inbox.

The danger, and it is a common one among capable people, is to treat the reset hour as a place to fix the entire system of life in one sitting. That ambition guarantees disappointment, then avoidance. A sustainable ritual has to accept the constraints of real weeks: interruptions, care needs, fatigue, and the simple fact that some items require longer blocks. The reset is not where those longer blocks happen. The reset is where they are named and given a home. There is a difference between handling something and deciding what will happen to it. The hour exists to create that difference reliably.

The path here is a set of design choices rather than a surge of effort. It begins with making the time and place sufficiently consistent that the session becomes automatic rather than an argument with oneself. It then turns to the tools, not as an invitation to optimise endlessly, but as a demand for a single calendar, a single task list, and a single capture place that can be trusted. From there the hour needs a flow with an internal logic, so that it does not drift into busywork or get hijacked by whatever feels most urgent in the moment. Finally, the hour needs an ending that is clean, because sustainability depends less on what is finished than on the knowledge that the session will not expand to eat the afternoon.

A quiet motif runs through all of this: the door. A ritual either has a clear doorway or it does not. When the doorway is unclear, people hover. They start and stop, step in and out, keep checking whether they are doing it correctly. When the doorway is clear, they enter, do the work that belongs there, and leave. Leaving matters. A reset that does not end teaches the mind that organising is endless, which makes organising aversive. A reset that ends teaches the mind that clarity has a boundary, which makes it easier to return next week.

The unresolved friction that pulls us into the practical work is not about motivation. It is about design honesty. When the intention to do a weekly reset meets the reality of your Sundays, what fails first: the time, the place, the tools, the sequence, or the refusal to stop?

Choosing a time and place

If the reset takes one hour, why does it so often feel impossible to begin? The paradox is not that people lack time. The paradox is that time exists, but only in slivers, and slivers are emotionally expensive. They require negotiation. They invite delay. They make every task compete with everything else, until even a simple act of getting organised starts to feel like an indulgence rather than maintenance. A weekly reset fails most often at the doorway, before any list is opened or any calendar is checked: the question of when, and where, becomes a silent argument with the week.

It usually starts well. Someone says, quietly, that Sunday will be the day. They can picture it. A calm table, a drink, a clear head. They might even enjoy the fantasy. Then Sunday arrives as Sundays do, carrying other people's needs, domestic noise, the lure of "just resting", the strange emotional weight of Monday on the horizon. The hour is postponed to the afternoon, then to the evening, then to "later". The mind does not stop thinking about it. It simply thinks about it with irritation. The ritual becomes negotiable, and negotiable habits do not survive contact with real life.

The decision is simple. Pick the slot.

That sentence sounds almost insulting, until one notices what it is really asking: not to find time, but to commit to a time that will not feel perfectly convenient. Consistency is not a reward for having an easy schedule; it is a tool for people whose schedules are messy. A consistent slot changes the nature of the task. It turns organising from a choice into a default. The brain likes defaults because defaults reduce decision fatigue. When the reset is a default, you do not have to persuade yourself each week that it is worth doing; you only have to show up and begin. When it is not a default, you have to argue for it repeatedly, and repeated argument is a form of attention leakage all by itself.

To see the difference, imagine two versions of the same person. In one version, they do the reset "when they get a chance". They scan the week whenever guilt spikes, or whenever something goes wrong, or whenever they have five minutes between other tasks. It feels flexible. It is also unstable. The mind cannot trust it, because the mind knows that five-minute scraps will be taken by whatever shouts loudest, and the reset requires quiet. The result is a familiar behaviour pattern: they keep reopening the same list, checking the same messages, mentally rehearsing the same upcoming commitments. Their planning becomes reactive. They pay for the reset in a hundred small interruptions rather than in one bounded session.

In the other version, the person has named a slot with enough regularity that it has become part of the week's architecture. The slot does not need to be romantic. It can be early before the house wakes, or late after it settles, or during a predictable lull. The point is that it happens. That simple reliability changes what "efficiency" means. Efficiency stops being speed and becomes fewer restarts. You can see it in behaviour: fewer frantic searches for details, fewer "I forgot" moments, fewer last-minute reschedules that cost social capital. The benefit is not that everything is perfect. The benefit is that the mind stops hovering, because it has learned that there is a reliable moment when the open loops will be gathered and decided.

Choosing a place works in the same way. It is tempting to wait for the ideal environment: a clean desk, silence, full focus, no interruptions. That environment exists for some people some weeks. For many, it does not. Waiting for ideal conditions turns the reset into a fair-weather practice, which means it disappears exactly when it is most needed. A place, like a time, is a default. When the place is consistent, the body learns the cue. The chair becomes a signal. The surface becomes a boundary. The headphones, if they are used, become a small ritual object: not a fashion statement, but a sign that attention is being protected for a short while. A kitchen table can do this job perfectly well. A desk can fail at it if the desk is also where you scroll, snack, and answer messages all day.

Place matters because it shapes the kind of attention you can bring. Attention is not only about will; it is also about context.

In one setting, you will be pulled into domestic micro-tasks, because the environment presents them: dishes, laundry, piles, people passing through. In another setting, you will be pulled into work micro-tasks, because the environment offers them: files, notifications, open documents. Neither setting is morally superior. Both have gravity. The job is to choose a place where the gravity is predictable enough that you can plan for it, rather than being constantly surprised by it. Predictability reduces the sense of risk. Risk, when it is felt, triggers monitoring. Monitoring turns into distraction. A reliable place does not eliminate distraction, but it limits the kind of distraction you must fight.

Consider a hypothetical researcher who tries to do the reset at the same workstation where they write and analyse data. The workstation is efficient for deep work, but it also carries the scent of unfinished projects: papers half-drafted, comments unanswered, datasets waiting. The moment they sit down, the mind begins to drift towards those gravitational fields. A task list becomes a doorway into work. The reset expands. It becomes a session of "catching up", which cannot be finished in an hour, which means the hour ends without closure, which means the mind learns that the reset is a trap. Now imagine the same person choosing a neutral place: a table used for meals, a corner of the library, a chair by the window with only a notebook and a calendar. The place does not solve the work. It simply prevents the reset from being hijacked by it. The difference is not comfort; it is containment.

Now consider a different hypothetical life: a parent whose Sundays are loud and unpredictable. There is no silence to be had. Children need things. The kitchen is active. The attempt to claim a perfect hour will fail, and the failure will be interpreted as personal weakness. Yet the constraint is not the person; it is the environment. In such a life, the honest choice may be a smaller, more protected pocket of time, and a place that creates a boundary even inside noise. Headphones can become that boundary. A closed door can become that boundary. A repeated phrase like "I am doing the weekly reset" can become that boundary, not as an announcement of virtue but as a signal that this hour is maintenance, like taking out the bins. The key is that the boundary is recognisable to others and to the self. A ritual that must be renegotiated each week will be lost. A ritual that has a clear cue stands a chance.

Here is the limitation that deserves respect: sometimes there is no stable slot. Shift work, irregular caregiving, unpredictable health demands, travel, and crisis periods can make weekly regularity feel like a cruel joke. In those seasons, forcing a rigid routine can create more stress than it relieves. The reconciliation is to aim for a stable *trigger* rather than a stable clock time. A trigger might be "after the last Sunday meal" or "once the household is in bed" or "before leaving the house for the week". The calendar might not allow a precise hour, but the week can still contain a doorway: a moment that reliably happens, even if its exact timing shifts. The success condition is not purity. It is repeatability. The chair, again, matters less than the cue that leads you to it.

Underlying all of this is a question of trust. Trust is not a feeling you summon; it is a system property you earn. You earn it by making a promise and keeping it often enough that the mind stops doubting. When time and place are unstable, the mind doubts. It keeps monitoring. It keeps pinging. It refuses to let go of open loops because it does not believe they will be handled later. When time and place are stable, the mind begins to release. You can observe the change in behaviour without any grand declarations: fewer frantic notes scribbled on scraps, fewer reminders set "just in case", fewer duplications across apps, fewer compulsive checks on Sunday evening because the reset has already happened. Trust is built from small, repeated proof.

There is also a subtle risk in choosing the "best" time and place: the risk of turning the reset into an identity project. If the slot is chosen because it looks impressive, it will be fragile.

If the place is chosen because it feels like the kind of place organised people use, it will be performative. The ritual must fit the life you have, not the life you wish you had. That requires a kind of adult humility. It means choosing a slot that may be slightly inconvenient but consistently available, and a place that may be ordinary but reliably bounded. It means accepting that the reset does not need to feel idyllic. It needs to happen.

The unresolved test is simple and slightly uncomfortable, because it forces contact with reality rather than aspiration: when you imagine doing the reset next week, what is the first point of resistance you feel in your body, and is it about the work itself or about the absence of a clear doorway into the hour?

Tools you actually need

If so many tools promise control, why does control so often slip away? The paradox is blunt: the more places you can put a commitment, the harder it becomes to know where it truly lives. The brain does not experience this as a tidy information-architecture problem. It experiences it as doubt. Doubt triggers checking. Checking becomes the new routine. A system meant to save attention quietly starts consuming it.

A clue comes from an unlikely place: GOV.UK, launched by the UK Government Digital Service in October 2012 in London, was built around a ruthless premise that citizens should not have to guess which of many sites holds the right answer (Government Digital Service, 2012). Consolidation was not a style choice. It was an operational decision to reduce duplication, dead ends, and conflicting versions. Personal organisation has the same enemy. It is not merely "forgetfulness". It is competing truths.

Choose one home for truth.

Tool sprawl begins innocently. A person captures ideas in a notes app because it is quick, uses email flags because they are already in the inbox, keeps a paper notebook because handwriting feels calmer, and stores dates in a calendar that syncs to some devices but not others. None of this is irrational. Each tool solves a small, local problem. The trouble appears later, in a moment of mild pressure. A meeting is rearranged. An appointment is moved. A deadline changes. The person updates one place but not the others, or cannot remember which place they updated, and now the week contains a contradiction. Contradictions are expensive. They force repeated checking, and repeated checking is the opposite of control.

The name for this is version conflict, a concept borrowed from any environment where information is edited across copies. In software development, teams guard against conflicting changes because conflicting changes create errors and rework. In life admin, conflicting changes create missed commitments and anxious monitoring. The visible behaviour is familiar: checking the calendar, then checking the email thread, then checking a text message, then checking a screenshot someone sent, then checking a note you wrote to yourself "just in case". The mind is not being obsessive for sport. It is compensating for an unreliable system. The implication is slightly ruthless: reliability matters more than features because reliability removes the need for vigilance.

A minimal toolset is not an aesthetic preference. It is risk management. The risk is concrete: turning up on the wrong day, missing a call, duplicating a task, failing to reply because you thought you already had. Each risk has a signature behaviour: double-booking, repeated searches, and the uncomfortable feeling of being behind even after you have "organised". A calendar is meant to prevent time collisions. A task list is meant to prevent forgotten actions. A capture place is meant to prevent ideas and obligations floating loose. When each of these exists in multiple places, you have not created redundancy; you have created disagreement.

Reliability requires a single source of truth for each category. That phrase can sound grand, but it describes something mundane: when you need to know when something happens, there is one calendar you trust without cross-checking. When you need to know what you have committed to do, there is one task list you consult without hunting through multiple apps. When something new arrives in your mind or in your life, there is one capture place where it goes by default. The goal is not to worship minimalism. The goal is to reduce the number of places your attention must patrol.

Consider what happens when the calendar is not singular. A person receives an invite, adds it to their work calendar, and later makes a personal plan without seeing the clash because their personal calendar is separate. Or they use two calendars for different contexts, and the boundary between contexts is porous, so the calendars need constant reconciliation. The "efficiency" cost appears as extra steps: duplicated entries, manual copying, periodic audits. The "risk" cost appears as collision: commitments that were technically recorded but practically invisible at the moment decisions were made. The implication is not that everyone must merge everything into one digital calendar. It is that whatever you call "the calendar" must be the place you consult before agreeing to anything time-specific. The measure is behavioural: do you check it, trust it, and act on it without needing a second verification?

Task lists breed even faster. A person keeps tasks in their inbox because it feels close to where requests arrive. They also keep tasks in a project tool because it feels professional. They also keep tasks in a notebook because it feels human. Each list is partially true. None is fully authoritative. The result is a peculiar kind of overload: not too many tasks, but too many representations of tasks. A task becomes an object that exists in multiple places, each requiring upkeep. This upkeep has a name in human factors research: cognitive load, the mental effort required to hold, update, and reconcile information. When the system is fragmented, cognitive load rises not because the tasks are harder, but because the bookkeeping is harder.

The capture place is the quiet hero of the minimal toolset because it protects the mind from an impossible job: remembering what it has not yet processed. Capturing is not organising. Capturing is collecting raw material so it stops living in working memory. When capture happens in multiple places, it creates an illusion of safety while increasing loss. Notes scatter across apps. Screenshots become a second inbox. Voice memos become a third. The mind senses this, even if the person pretends not to. It responds by keeping more in the head, "just in case". That is the opposite of what capture is meant to achieve.

Here the motif sharpens: the master copy. Every time you create a second copy of a commitment, you create a second master in your own mind, and masters disagree. People do not suffer because they have no tools. People suffer because they have too many half-trusted tools. Half-trust is the worst state because it triggers constant monitoring. A fully trusted notebook can be enough. A fully trusted app can be enough. A mixture of partly trusted systems produces the internal equivalent of a committee meeting: no one is sure who has authority, so everyone keeps speaking.

A checkable example from outside personal life shows how costly such confusion can be. On 23 September 1999, NASA lost the Mars Climate Orbiter, with investigations pointing to a mismatch in units used by different teams as a contributing factor (NASA, 1999). The detail is famous because it is so small, and because the consequences were so large. The deeper point is structural: when systems exchange information without a single, agreed representation, errors become more likely. Personal organisation is not spaceflight, but it runs on the same principle. When your systems disagree about what is due, where it is stored, and what has been decided, attention becomes your error-correction mechanism. It keeps checking because it has learned that unchecked assumptions are dangerous.

The temptation at this point is to chase tool perfection: to search for the app that will finally solve everything, to migrate again, to start fresh, to build a new taxonomy of tags. That is a familiar form of avoidance dressed in competence. It feels like progress because it is effortful and measurable. Yet it often produces more fragmentation, because each migration creates leftovers: old lists you do not quite delete, documents in the wrong place, a lingering fear that something important remains behind in the previous system. Migration is sometimes necessary. It is also risky. The implication is not "never change tools". It is to treat tool changes as significant events rather than as harmless experiments, because they create long tails of uncertainty that feed the very attention leakage you are trying to stop.

A more realistic approach is to treat the toolset as infrastructure rather than identity. Infrastructure should be boring. It should work when you are tired. It should work when you are distracted. It should work when you are in a hurry. Features are seductive because they promise mastery, but mastery is not the requirement. The requirement is that you can put something in, retrieve it later, and trust that it will still mean what you intended. Trust here can be measured. If you frequently duplicate tasks across systems to feel safe, you do not trust the system. If you frequently keep messages unread to remind yourself, you do not trust the system. If you frequently screenshot details "just in case", you do not trust the system. Those behaviours are not personal quirks; they are diagnostics.

Research on task switching offers a useful lens on why tool sprawl feels so draining. Rubinstein, Meyer, and Evans found that switching between tasks can impose costs in time and accuracy, even when tasks are relatively simple (Rubinstein, Meyer, and Evans, 2001). Tool sprawl increases switching. It forces you to move between contexts not because your life genuinely requires it, but because your information is distributed. Every switch invites distraction. Every switch invites a new open loop. The implication is not to become puritanical about single-tasking. The implication is to reduce unnecessary switching by reducing the number of places where key commitments might be hiding.

A credible limitation needs to be faced honestly: sometimes multiple toolsets are unavoidable. Some workplaces require certain systems. Some people must keep personal and professional information separate for privacy or safety. Some roles involve compliance requirements that dictate where records must live. In such cases, insisting on a single universal tool is not only unrealistic, it can be irresponsible. The reconciliation is to preserve the principle without insisting on the simplest form. You can have separate domains, but each domain must still have its own master copy. If there is a work calendar, it must be the work calendar. If there is a personal calendar, it must be the personal calendar. The danger is not separation; it is ambiguity about where the authoritative record sits. Ambiguity is what produces the anxious cross-checking.

Notice how the minimal set of tools maps to the kinds of failures described earlier in this book. Open loops persist when there is no trusted container. Tiny tasks balloon when information is missing or scattered. Perfectionism bites when the system is unreliable and the person compensates by overchecking and overrecording. A single calendar reduces time ambiguity. A single task list reduces action ambiguity. A single capture place reduces input ambiguity. Together, they reduce the need for the mind to play courier and auditor.

The master copy motif returns as a quiet standard. When you hear yourself think, "Where did I put that?", the question is not merely about storage. It is about authority. Where is the authoritative place for this kind of thing? When you find yourself updating the same detail in multiple places, the question is not how to be more diligent. It is why the system tolerates multiple masters. When you feel the itch to add a new app, the question is not whether the app is clever. It is whether the app will reduce monitoring or increase it.

A system that is reliable is often plain. It may even feel slightly underpowered compared to the glittering alternatives. That is a feature, not a flaw. The most valuable outcome of a minimal toolset is not aesthetic simplicity; it is the reduction of background stress. You can see it in the small quietness that follows a decision properly recorded. You can feel it when you stop checking. You can notice it when you sit down on a Sunday and the information you need is where it should be, not because you are unusually disciplined, but because you have removed the conditions that force you to rely on discipline.

The forward test is not whether your tools are impressive. It is whether they are trusted. When a new commitment arrives, where does it go without debate, and when you need the truth quickly, which single place do you consult without cross-checking another?

The four-part reset flow

In Houston in April 1970, a room full of engineers learned a hard lesson about sequence. Apollo 13 had suffered an explosion en route to the Moon, and the job became brutally simple: keep three people alive and get them home. The work was not a single heroic insight. It was a disciplined choreography of information. Data was gathered, checked against what had already happened, turned into decisions, and translated into actions that could be executed under constraint. The order mattered because the wrong order produces noise. Noise wastes time. Time was scarce.

Sequence is mercy.

The same principle governs a far quieter domain: the hour set aside to regain control of a week. The hour does not fail because the tasks are too numerous. It fails because the mind is asked to do incompatible kinds of work at once. It tries to collect loose inputs while simultaneously judging them. It tries to remember last week while simultaneously planning next week. It tries to make decisions while still swimming in unprocessed information. This is how an organising session turns into busywork: not because the person is foolish, but because the cognitive demands are conflicting. When the brain is forced to mix collection, evaluation, and planning in a single undifferentiated swirl, it defaults to the easiest behaviour available, which is often tidying, rearranging, and hovering.

The trade-off is simple and exacting. A free-form session feels flexible, but flexibility invites drift. A structured flow can feel restrictive, but restriction creates containment. The point of a four-part flow is not to make the reset rigid; it is to make it *finishable*. It gives the hour a shape that the mind can recognise, and that recognition reduces the urge to keep checking, keep tweaking, keep searching for the perfect way to do it. A contained hour does not demand constant self-management. It moves forward.

The first movement, capture, exists because uncollected inputs sabotage everything that follows. Capture is the act of moving loose obligations out of the mind and into a single place where they can be seen. The scene is mundane: a person pulls together scraps of paper, screenshots, half-written notes, messages flagged but not answered, stray reminders typed into odd corners of apps. What is happening underneath is more important. The mind is being relieved of its role as storage. Working memory is not built to be an attic. When capture is skipped, the mind continues to ping, interrupting later thinking with "don't forget" alarms. Those alarms feel like urgency, but they are often just evidence of poor collection. The implication is direct: if you try to make decisions before you have gathered the inputs, you will keep revisiting the same material in scattered bursts, and the hour will be consumed by re-discovery rather than progress.

A visible metric helps here, because abstractions can flatter us. If capture is working, you can point to where the truth sits: a single inbox, a single page, a single list. You can also notice a behavioural change: fewer tabs left open as placeholders, fewer unread messages kept as reminders, fewer "I will remember this" promises made to yourself. These are not personality traits. They are system effects. The person becomes less vigilant, not because they care less, but because the system is now doing some of the remembering. That is the whole point of a reset.

The second movement, review, exists because raw inputs without context turn into overreaction. Review is where the past week is scanned quickly enough to stay honest and briefly enough to avoid rumination. Without this step, the mind treats every unprocessed item as potentially critical, because it lacks a map of what has already happened and what has slipped. Review provides that map. It is the difference between reading a message in isolation and reading it with knowledge of the week it belongs to. A rescheduling request feels different when you remember the appointment was already moved once. A nagging task feels different when you remember it depends on a response you have not received. Review is where the system stops guessing.

This is also where a great deal of "efficiency" is either gained or lost. The most common failure mode is to confuse review with editing. Editing is seductive. It creates clean lines. Review is less flattering. It confronts the reality of what did and did not happen, and it exposes patterns without dramatising them. The implication is uncomfortable but useful: a person who skips review tends to repeat the same planning mistakes because they never pause long enough to see what their week actually does. They plan as if they were a different person with a different schedule. Review corrects the fantasy.

The third movement, decide, exists because information without commitments is merely organised anxiety. This is the pivot from knowing to choosing. Deciding is where ambiguous items are turned into stable outcomes: scheduled, delegated, deleted, parked, or converted into a next action that can be done in one sitting. The risk of skipping this step is easy to observe. People can spend a full hour collecting and reviewing and still feel no lighter, because nothing has been settled. The mind continues to monitor. The ping continues. Decisions close loops. They do not need to be perfect decisions. They need to be decisions that reduce repeated thinking.

This is where the earlier theme of "tiny tasks" reveals its practical bite. Many items that look small cannot be decided until a missing detail is found or a criterion is chosen. Deciding is therefore not always the act of completing; it is often the act of making something runnable. You can see the difference in language. A vague intention remains vague. A clear next action has edges. The person is no longer carrying a foggy obligation; they are carrying a concrete step. The implication is that a decision does not have to solve the entire problem to reduce attention leakage. It has to stabilise the next move.

The fourth movement, prepare, exists because decisions that do not reach the calendar and task list remain theoretical. Preparation translates commitments into a week that can hold them. It includes time boundaries, buffers, and the reality that certain tasks demand certain kinds of attention. Preparation is not a fantasy schedule. It is an arrangement of constraints so that Monday does not begin with improvisation. The visible behaviour here is not grand. It is the absence of franticness. A person begins the week without needing to search for the basic facts of their own commitments. They can open one calendar and trust it. They can consult one task list and act. The implication is practical: preparation prevents the week from becoming a series of emergency micro-plans created under stress.

A quiet motif can help unify this, because the whole flow is about movement without drift. Think of the reset hour as a conveyor belt. Items are placed on it. They move past a small set of stations. At each station, a specific kind of work happens, and then the item moves on. When people try to do everything at once, they pull items off the belt and scatter them across the floor, then spend the hour stepping over them. Capture is loading the belt. Review is the first scan, checking what each item is in relation to the week that produced it. Decide is the sorting station where each item is given a fate. Prepare is the packing station where what remains is placed into the week ahead in a form that can be executed. The belt image matters because it disciplines attention. It limits the temptation to pick up the shiniest or most emotionally charged item and treat it as the whole session.

There is a reason order matters beyond personal preference. Each step reduces a different kind of uncertainty, and uncertainty is the fuel of mental noise. Capture reduces uncertainty about what exists. Review reduces uncertainty about context and recency. Decide reduces uncertainty about what will happen next. Prepare reduces uncertainty about when actions will occur and how they will fit. If you attempt to prepare before you decide, you create a schedule full of provisional placeholders that demand constant revision. If you decide before you review, you make choices based on incomplete context and then undo them later. If you review before you capture, you are reviewing a partial dataset and will keep discovering new inputs that destabilise your choices. The implication is not that you must be obsessive. It is that sequence reduces rework.

A second checkable example, far from personal planning, shows why structured sequence beats heroic memory when stakes are high. The World Health Organization introduced the Surgical Safety Checklist in 2008, with the aim of standardising critical checks around surgery (World Health Organization, 2008). Whatever one thinks about the wider debates around checklists, the underlying logic is relevant: complex work benefits from a small sequence that forces essential information to be gathered and confirmed before irreversible actions occur. The checklist is not intelligence replaced by bureaucracy. It is intelligence protected from omission. The relevance to a weekly reset is not that life admin is surgery. It is that life admin has its own version of omission risk: the missed appointment, the forgotten follow-up, the duplicated commitment, the quiet promise made to someone that evaporates because it was never placed into the systems that govern behaviour.

Still, there is a limitation that must be faced to keep the flow honest. Some weeks are dominated by interruption and volatility: urgent care needs, crisis at work, travel disruption, a sudden family demand. In those weeks, the neat sequence can be interrupted, and insisting on purity can create more frustration than clarity. There is also a different limitation for certain kinds of intellectual work. Research and creative thinking sometimes benefit from nonlinear movement, where reflection and decision intermingle, and where forcing a decision too early can reduce quality. The reconciliation is to distinguish between the reset hour and the work the reset supports. The reset hour is a logistics ritual, not an innovation workshop. It exists to stabilise commitments and reduce attention leakage. It can tolerate minor deviation when reality demands it, but it cannot tolerate losing its purpose. When the flow bends, it should bend in a way that still protects containment: keep collecting inputs, keep making decisions explicit, keep translating commitments into a form the week can hold.

The flow also guards against a subtler enemy: the temptation to confuse organising with feeling organised. Busywork thrives in the gaps where sequence is missing. People polish their lists because polishing feels controllable. They colour-code because colour is reassuring. They rename categories because renaming provides a sense of mastery. Meanwhile, the actual decisions remain untouched. The conveyor belt stops. Items pile up. The mind continues to monitor the unresolved. A clear flow makes this harder to do because it keeps asking a plain question at each station: is this input collected, is its context understood, has its fate been decided, has it been placed into the week? These questions are not inspiring. They are effective.

A reliable flow also creates an ending, which matters more than most people admit. When the hour ends without a clear sense of having moved items through the stations, the mind learns a nasty lesson: organising is endless, therefore dangerous. It starts avoiding the ritual, or performing it in superficial ways that do not threaten to expand. A contained flow, by contrast, teaches the mind that the session can start and stop safely. That safety is a form of trust. Trust reduces monitoring. Monitoring is what people are trying to escape.

The forward test is therefore not whether the four words sound neat. It is whether the sequence produces less rework and fewer compulsive checks across the week. When the next Sunday arrives, will you sit down and begin by loading the belt, or will you reach for the most emotionally urgent item and let it hijack the hour before anything has been gathered?

Setting boundaries and endings

On 15 January 2009, when US Airways Flight 1549 lost power in both engines after a bird strike, Chesley Sullenberger and Jeffrey Skiles did not have the luxury of finishing every thought. They had minutes to act, and their decisions had to respect a boundary set by physics: altitude, speed, distance, water. The story is often told as calm heroism, but the more instructive detail is harsher. They did not try to do everything. They did what the moment could hold, then committed. A boundary was not a failure of ambition. It was the condition of survival.

Boundaries protect the work.

A weekly reset is not a cockpit emergency, but it faces a quieter version of the same dilemma: there will always be more to do than the hour can contain. If the hour becomes a place where everything must be resolved, it will be avoided. If it becomes a place where time limits are ignored, it will expand until it steals the very rest and life it is meant to support. The problem is not that there is more. The problem is what "more" does to attention when it has no agreed endpoint. Without an ending, the mind refuses to relax. It keeps scanning, keeps tweaking, keeps reopening. The reset becomes another open loop.

A clean ending is therefore not a flourish. It is the core mechanism that makes the ritual repeatable. Repeatability matters because trust is built through recurrence: the mind learns that a certain hour exists, that it begins in a certain way, and crucially, that it ends. When it ends cleanly, the mind can let go of what remains because it has a designated place to put it. When it does not end cleanly, the mind learns that organising is an endless trap, and it responds like any sensible organism: it resists entering the trap. The avoidance that follows is not laziness. It is conditioned response to past overrun.

The first way the hour overruns is through moral confusion. People treat the reset as a test of worthiness, a chance to "catch up" and restore a fantasy of being on top of everything. Catch up is a seductive phrase because it implies a finish line. For most adult lives, there is no finish line. There is only maintenance and occasional repair. When the hour is framed as a rescue operation, it becomes emotionally charged, and emotional charge makes it hard to stop. Stopping feels like failure. Yet stopping is the design. The reset is not where you solve every problem; it is where you reduce attention leakage and create a workable week. The implication is simple: the hour must be bounded even if the list is not.

The second way the hour overruns is through attention capture. Certain tasks have a gravitational pull. A financial form with missing information. A complex email thread. A household repair that requires comparisons. A relationship issue that cannot be "processed" in a quick sitting. These items do not merely take time; they change the nature of the session. The mind falls into problem-solving mode, and problem-solving mode is expansive. It is also self-rewarding. It produces the feeling of being serious. Meanwhile, the rest of the reset stalls. Inputs remain unprocessed. Decisions remain unmade. The session becomes lopsided, and because it is lopsided, it cannot end cleanly. The person either overruns to compensate or stops with a sense of incompletion that discourages returning next week. The risk is not wasted minutes. The risk is the collapse of the ritual itself.

This is where the idea of a "parking list" earns its keep. The parking list is not procrastination with a nicer label. It is a boundary tool: a place where items that require a different kind of time are held without being allowed to hijack the hour. The behaviour is observable. When a complex item appears, instead of diving into it, the person records it in a dedicated place and assigns it a future context: a longer session, a separate project plan, a specific slot in the week if appropriate. The item is not ignored. It is contained. The implication is that containment can be a form of action. It converts a task from "haunting the week" to "scheduled for proper attention". That shift reduces the mental ping because it answers the brain's most basic question: what happens next?

A named example outside personal organisation can make this logic feel less like self-help and more like human factors engineering. The World Health Organization's Surgical Safety Checklist, introduced in 2008, is built around deliberate pauses and handovers (World Health Organization, 2008). The checklist does not attempt to include every nuance of a surgical case. It enforces critical moments of verification and shared understanding. That is a boundary. It acknowledges that not everything can be covered in one sweep, and it protects the process by insisting on certain closure points. The relevance here is not the clinical domain. It is the principle: complex work becomes safer and more repeatable when it includes explicit stop points, not merely start points.

Boundaries also prevent a subtler failure: cosmetic completion. People can keep organising indefinitely and still avoid the decisive actions that would make the week runnable. They rewrite tasks. They reorder. They polish. They drift into what feels like productive tidying, and because there is no ending, there is no moment when decisions must be committed. An ending forces commitment. It creates a deadline within the hour. Deadlines can be stressful, but in this context the stress is functional: it stops the mind from indulging in infinite refinement. It shifts the focus from "make it perfect" to "make it stable". Stability reduces attention leakage. Stability is the goal.

The psychology of stopping is also tangled with what researchers call the sunk cost effect: the tendency to continue an endeavour because of what has already been invested, rather than because it is still the best use of resources (Arkes and Blumer, 1985). In a reset session, sunk cost shows up like this: "I have already spent most of the hour, so I should keep going until it feels done." The feeling of "done" is elusive precisely because life is not a closed system. The hour can always be extended. The implication is that an intentional stop is not merely time management; it is a cognitive correction. It refuses to be seduced by past investment. It treats the boundary as non-negotiable, which paradoxically increases the likelihood of returning next week because the mind trusts that the ritual will not eat the day.

A credible limitation must be admitted. Some weeks genuinely require longer admin sessions. Life events, deadlines, complex travel, moving house, caregiving crises, major work submissions, and bureaucratic tangles can demand more than an hour. Pretending otherwise is naive. The reconciliation is that the weekly reset does not forbid longer sessions; it protects them. It creates the clarity to identify which items need a longer block and to assign them properly, rather than letting them spill across the week in anxious fragments. The weekly reset is the place where you decide that a longer session is needed and where you make that need explicit. That act, by itself, can reduce background stress because it replaces vague dread with a named plan.

A boundary also has a social dimension. People share space. They share Sundays. An unbounded organising ritual can quietly take over a household because it expands into the afternoon, then into the evening, then into the emotional bandwidth of everyone nearby. It creates irritability and distraction. An hour that ends cleanly is easier to respect, both by the person doing it and by the people around them, because it behaves like a defined commitment rather than a vague absence. That respect matters for sustainability. A ritual that repeatedly causes conflict will be abandoned or hidden. Neither outcome supports control.

The motif that holds this subchapter together is the landing. You do not need to finish the entire journey; you need to land the plane. Landing means closing enough loops that the week can begin without chaos. Landing means ensuring the calendar is trustworthy, the task list is runnable, and the unhandled items have a safe container rather than being left as fog. Landing means leaving the session with a sense of completion that is real: not the completion of all tasks, but the completion of the reset itself. A clean landing teaches the mind, week after week, that organising is finite. Finite rituals are sustainable. Infinite rituals are not.

A clean ending also protects attention in the hours after the reset. Without an ending, the mind keeps returning to what was left open, not because it is irresponsible, but because it has not received a clear signal that the session is complete. People then find themselves half-organising through the evening: rechecking, adding items, reopening the calendar, trying to patch the feeling of incompletion. This behaviour is a clue. It suggests the session did not truly end, and without a true end there is no true rest. The implication is that the ending is not a small procedural detail. It is the gateway between planning and living.

The forward test is deliberately awkward, because boundaries are easiest to admire and hardest to enforce: when the hour reaches its limit and a large, emotionally charged item is still unresolved, will you extend the session to soothe the discomfort, or will you create a parking place robust enough that you can stop and still trust what happens next?

Chapter 3
Fast capture for scattered thoughts

A person stands at the sink, hands in warm water, and remembers something that cannot be remembered later. It is not a life-changing insight. It is a small obligation with sharp edges: a message to send, a form to return, an idea for a meeting, a household task that will matter at the wrong moment if it is forgotten. The mind reacts the way it always does when it senses a loose end. It repeats the thought. It rehearses it. It tries to keep it afloat while the body continues with the ordinary business of the evening. A minute later another thought arrives, unrelated, equally insistent. The brain becomes a juggling act performed with wet hands.

Later, the person tries to be sensible. They make a note. But where? A note app already holds fragments. A chat to self is used for quick reminders. Email drafts have become a parking area. Screenshots sit in a camera roll like unlabelled parcels. A paper notebook exists somewhere, half used. The act of capture, meant to reduce cognitive load, becomes another decision. They postpone the decision and promise to remember instead. The promise is made with confidence and broken with predictable regularity. The result is not simply forgetting. It is background monitoring. The mind, aware that capture is unreliable, keeps pinging.

This is the central discomfort: the human mind is excellent at generating concerns and surprisingly poor at storing them cleanly. It can create ideas at inconvenient times with impressive creativity, but it cannot be trusted to hold a growing inventory of tasks without cost. When capture is fragmented, the mind behaves as if nothing is safe. It repeats itself. It checks. It interrupts. The person begins to live inside a low-grade internal notification system, where the volume rises whenever they are tired or busy. The irony is sharp. The more we need to capture quickly, the more complicated we make capture, until the whole act becomes negotiable and therefore inconsistent.

The trade-off is not between being reflective and being efficient. It is between capturing quickly enough to reduce mental noise and capturing expansively enough to satisfy an impulse towards completeness. A capture practice that turns into journalling will be avoided by anyone with a full life. A capture practice that is too sparse will fail to relieve pressure because it will not feel trustworthy. The aim is a fast, neutral collection of inputs, without judgement, without sorting, and without the temptation to solve everything in the moment. Capture must be light enough to do when life is noisy, and solid enough that the mind believes it.

The stakes are immediate and quietly serious. When scattered thoughts are not captured reliably, they do not simply vanish. They reappear as interruption, which degrades the quality of everything else. Focused work becomes porous. Conversations become half-present. Rest becomes restless because the brain uses quiet moments to rehearse what it fears will be forgotten. People sometimes misinterpret this as anxiety about life itself, when it is often anxiety about storage. The mind is trying to prevent loss. Its method is crude: repeated reminders. A dependable capture practice lowers the need for that method, which means attention can return to the present without feeling irresponsible.

There is also a longer-term cost. When capture is unreliable, people begin to mistrust their own intentions. They stop making commitments to themselves because those commitments are not honoured reliably. They also start to overcompensate: excessive reminders, duplicated notes, messages left unread as crude flags, a constant sense of being behind even when much has been accomplished. This is not overthinking as a personality trait. It is a rational response to an environment where information is not contained. A single trusted capture place changes this relationship. It creates one queue rather than many hiding spots, and a queue can be processed. Hiding spots cannot.

The motif here is the pocket. A pocket is meant to hold things safely until you need them. When your notes live in ten pockets, you spend your day patting yourself down to check what you might have lost. You do it without thinking. You do it while walking, while waiting, while trying to concentrate. One good pocket does not make you perfect. It makes you calmer, because you stop searching your own attention for items that should be stored elsewhere.

The path forward begins by making one inbox the default destination for anything that would otherwise rattle around in the mind or scatter across devices. It then relies on a brief, honest clearing of the head that prioritises relief over elegance, allowing the raw inventory of obligations and ideas to be captured without being weighed, judged, or translated into a perfect system. The movement is from scattered to contained, from internal monitoring to external holding, from repeated rehearsal to a single place where the truth can wait its turn.

The friction that pulls us into the practical work is specific enough to be diagnostic. When a thought arrives at an inconvenient time, do you know exactly where it would go without debate, or does the debate itself become the reason the thought stays lodged in your head?

Building a single inbox

In 1971, at Bolt, Beranek and Newman in Cambridge, Massachusetts, Ray Tomlinson sent a message between two computers on the ARPANET and chose the @ symbol to separate user from host. The technical details matter less here than the cultural accident: a new kind of container was born, a place where messages could arrive and wait. The modern inbox is so familiar it is almost invisible, yet its underlying promise remains radical. Things can be received without being handled immediately. They can be held somewhere other than the mind.

One tray. Everything lands there.

That simplicity is precisely what most personal capture systems quietly lack. Life now produces inputs in strange forms: a screenshot of an address, a fleeting thought in the shower, a voice memo taken while walking, a message half-read on a crowded train, a paper slip from a school bag, a confirmation buried in an email thread, a photo of a parking sign taken as a reminder. Each input feels too small to dignify with a "system", so it gets tucked into whatever pocket is nearest. The pockets multiply. Notes scatter across devices. Reminders live as drafts. Screenshots become a shadow inbox. The mind, sensing fragmentation, keeps a second copy internally by rehearsing. That rehearsal is the beginning of background stress.

The central claim is blunt: multiple capture spots create the *illusion* of organisation while increasing loss. The illusion comes from activity. A person writes things down, takes screenshots, flags messages, scribbles notes on paper. The mind observes the busyness and assumes some form of control. The loss arrives later, when a detail is needed and no one can remember where it was stored. The result is not only wasted search time. It is mistrust. Mistrust changes behaviour. People begin to duplicate capture in multiple places "just in case", or they avoid capture altogether because the act of choosing where to put something becomes its own small burden. The implication is that a scattered capture system does not merely fail to reduce cognitive load; it adds a new layer of monitoring.

The first scene is familiar to anyone whose life crosses multiple contexts. A professional receives a message about rescheduling an appointment. They are in the middle of something, so they mark it unread and move on. Later, they remember the appointment and search their inbox. It is not there. It was a text. Or it was in a work chat. Or it was in a calendar notification they dismissed. Now they search across channels, and in searching they stumble into other obligations, each one generating fresh open loops. This is not a lack of intelligence. It is a predictable outcome of poor containment. The concept here is a single source of truth for capture: one place where new inputs go before they are processed. The implication is practical. When capture has one home, attention stops acting as a search engine.

The mind's insistence on a single home is not an aesthetic preference; it is a cognitive requirement. Unprocessed inputs behave like open loops. They trigger intrusions, mental pings, and repeated checking, particularly when the person suspects that something might be lost. Evidence from goal and task research suggests that uncompleted intentions can keep resurfacing and that making a plan can reduce intrusive thoughts (Masicampo and Baumeister, 2011). The detail worth holding onto is not the laboratory framing; it is the mechanism. When the mind cannot trust an external container, it compensates by keeping items active internally. That compensation has a cost: it competes with focused thinking, rest, and the ability to be fully present.

A single inbox works by making capture frictionless and retrieval predictable. Frictionless capture matters because scattered thoughts arrive at inconvenient times; if the capture method requires choosing among multiple locations, the brain postpones the choice and tries to remember instead. Predictable retrieval matters because the mind only relaxes when it knows where something will be found later. This is why the form of the inbox matters less than its authority. It could be digital or paper. It could be a notes app, a task app, or a physical in-tray. What matters is that it is the default destination for anything not already in the right place. The visible behaviour of a system with an authoritative inbox is simple: fewer "where did I put that?" moments, fewer duplicate reminders, fewer screenshots taken as a substitute for decisions.

A second checkable example shows how the inbox became a cultural object rather than a mere technical feature. On 1 April 2004, Google launched Gmail, framing email around a searchable archive rather than a fragile, folder-obsessed filing cabinet. Whatever one thinks of the attention costs of email itself, Gmail's popularity reinforced a broader idea: a large volume of incoming items can remain in one place and still be manageable if retrieval is reliable. Search replaced obsessive sorting as the primary method of finding information. The implication for personal capture is not "just search everything". It is that a single queue becomes workable when it is trusted. Trust reduces the urge to scatter.

The moment a person tries to build a single inbox, the resistance usually appears in the form of identity and anxiety. Identity says, "I am a notebook person." Anxiety says, "What if I lose it?" Both responses point to the same underlying need: a container that feels safe enough to offload into. Safety is not mystical. It is produced by repeated retrieval. When a system repeatedly returns what was captured, the mind stops clenching. When a system sometimes loses items, or makes them hard to find, the mind compensates with vigilance. The metric is behavioural. Vigilance looks like double-capturing, keeping messages unread, leaving tabs open, and carrying reminders in the head even after writing them down. The goal of a single inbox is not aesthetic tidiness. It is the reduction of vigilance.

Tool sprawl undermines this by introducing version conflict at the level of capture. A thought is captured in one app. Another thought goes into a different app because that one was open. A screenshot is taken "temporarily" and then becomes permanent. A paper note is made and then forgotten on a desk. Each capture method is individually plausible. Together, they create a problem of authority. Where does the mind look when it needs the truth? If the answer is "it depends", attention begins to patrol, and patrolling is exhausting. This is why even a very sophisticated set of tools can produce more stress than a single, humble inbox: sophistication increases choice; choice increases hesitation; hesitation increases internal storage.

There is, however, a credible limitation that deserves respect. Some domains require separation. A person may have workplace compliance rules, sensitive research data, or privacy boundaries that make a single universal inbox unrealistic or undesirable. Others have roles that generate a high volume of incoming requests where triage must begin immediately, not because of personal preference but because other people's work depends on it. In such cases, insisting on one container for everything can be naive. The reconciliation is to preserve the principle of authority without pretending that all inputs belong together. A person can maintain separate domains and still have a single inbox *within each domain*, or a single capture inbox that holds personal reminders while work systems handle work tickets. The enemy is not separation. The enemy is ambiguity about where capture is supposed to happen when the thought arrives.

A single inbox also risks becoming a comfort object if it is treated as a vault rather than a queue. The point is not to store everything indefinitely. The point is to create a place where raw inputs can wait without consuming attention, so they can later be reviewed and converted into decisions. When the inbox becomes a permanent dumping ground, trust collapses again, because the mind learns that capture does not lead to clarity. This failure mode is common among intelligent people precisely because they can tolerate complexity. They can live with a messy inbox for a long time. The cost shows up elsewhere: the returning ping, the recurring sense of "something I am missing", the impulse to keep creating new capture methods rather than facing the backlog in the existing one. The implication is that a single inbox does not solve anything by itself. It creates the conditions for solving: one queue, one place to look, one set of items awaiting processing.

The quiet motif that unifies this is the tray. A tray is not a museum display. It is a staging area. The tray's job is to hold things temporarily so they stop being held mentally, and to make the next action easier because everything that needs attention is visible in one place. When capture is scattered, life becomes a series of scavenger hunts. When capture is centralised, life becomes a queue. Queues are not glamorous, but they are sane. They allow prioritisation. They allow completion. They allow an ending.

The most revealing test of whether a single inbox exists is not theoretical. It shows itself in micro-moments. A new obligation arrives while a person is busy. Do they know, without debate, where it belongs? Do they capture it once and move on, or do they keep it spinning in their head because they do not trust any single container? The answer predicts whether the mind will relax during the week or keep patrolling for losses. The discomfort at the heart of this subchapter is therefore a forward-facing diagnostic question: when the next stray thought hits, where will it land, and will that landing be decisive enough that the thought stops pinging?

Clearing your head quickly

In 1986 at Southern Methodist University in Dallas, psychologist James W. Pennebaker published research on expressive writing that made an unfashionable point: putting thoughts into words can change how the mind carries them (Pennebaker and Beall, 1986). The work is often discussed in the context of emotion, but it also illuminates a plainer phenomenon that shows up in any crowded week. When concerns remain unarticulated, they behave like background processes. They interrupt. They recur. They sap attention at inconvenient moments. When they are externalised, even crudely, the mind can stop guarding them quite so tightly.

The relief is not poetic. It is mechanical. A person sits down intending to focus and instead finds their attention repeatedly snagged by reminders that arrive without invitation: an email that needs a reply, a form that is half done, a promise made in passing, a thought that feels too important to forget. The mind keeps turning its head towards the same unresolved things, as if checking that they are still there. It is a form of monitoring, and monitoring is exhausting because it offers no closure, only reassurance for a few minutes before the doubt returns.

Put it down, not off.

That sentence captures the aim. Clearing the head quickly is not a confessional exercise and not a search for insight. It is the deliberate act of moving obligations and loose thoughts out of working memory and into a single place where they can be handled later. The distinction matters because intelligent people often sabotage capture by turning it into self-analysis. They begin to write and, within moments, the page becomes a stage for judgement: why am I like this, why can I not keep on top of it, what does this say about me. The brain dump becomes a narrative. Narratives are endless. The point here is not to understand the whole story of your life. The point is to stop your attention leaking through a hundred tiny cracks.

A fast brain dump works because it respects the limitations of the mind. Working memory is designed for immediate reasoning, not for storing an ever-growing inventory of commitments. When it is overloaded, the mind compensates by pinging you with reminders. Those reminders often feel like anxiety, but they are also a primitive safety system: if something is not stored reliably elsewhere, the mind keeps it active. Research by Masicampo and Baumeister suggests that unfulfilled goals increase intrusive thoughts and that forming a plan can reduce those intrusions (Masicampo and

Baumeister, 2011). The important insight is not that plans are magical. It is that the mind quietens when it has evidence that a concern has been captured and given a fate, even if that fate is simply "this will be dealt with later".

The core skill, then, is neutral capture. Neutral capture treats thoughts as inputs rather than as verdicts. It records what needs recording without deciding, in that moment, whether it is silly, important, overdue, shameful, or ambitious. This neutrality is not a philosophical stance. It is a practical one. Judgement slows capture, because judgement invites argument. Argument triggers avoidance. Avoidance keeps the item in the head. Neutrality keeps the pen moving, or the keys tapping, or the voice note rolling, and movement matters because the whole purpose is to drain the mind's holding tank quickly, not to refine the contents.

The scene that makes this most obvious is the start of a Sunday reset hour. Someone sits down with the intention of getting organised and immediately feels a surge of internal noise: "I must not forget," "I should have done," "I need to sort." If they begin to review their calendar or task list straight away, the noise competes with the review and contaminates it. They keep jumping to whatever feels most urgent or most emotionally charged. The result is a familiar kind of busywork, where they touch many things but settle few. A brain dump before review changes the order of operations. It lowers the background volume so the later decisions can be made with a clearer head. The implication is simple: the brain dump is not the organising. It is the precondition for organising.

A quiet motif helps because this practice is easy to misunderstand. Think of the brain dump as a scratchpad. A scratchpad is not the final draft. It is where you put the raw material so it stops hovering. The scratchpad is allowed to be messy. In fact, it should be messy. The only failure mode is to treat the scratchpad as a place where everything must already be tidy and meaningful. That turns capture into performance.

Performance invites procrastination. A scratchpad invites speed.

Speed matters because the mind is opportunistic. If capture takes too long, it will start sorting and solving prematurely. It will see a task and begin planning it. It will see an emotional concern and begin rehearsing the conversation. It will see a complex admin item and begin searching for documents. Those moves can be useful at the right time. They are corrosive during capture. They turn a quick unloading into a sprawling session, and sprawling sessions are precisely what time-conscious people cannot sustain. The practice being described is therefore less about thoroughness and more about containment: capture quickly enough that the mind cannot bargain its way into avoidance or perfectionism.

Neutral capture also addresses a particular trap for researchers and thoughtful professionals: the blending of tasks and ideas. Some inputs are obligations. Others are intellectual sparks. Both can create mental pings, but they require different handling later. The brain dump does not need to separate them. It needs to *collect* them so they stop competing with whatever you are doing. This is where a single inbox, established earlier, becomes essential. Without a single destination, the brain dump itself becomes fragmented: some items go into a notebook, others into a notes app, others into screenshots, others into messages to yourself. Fragmentation brings back version conflict, and version conflict brings back monitoring. A scratchpad that lands in one trusted place converts scattered attention into a queue.

There is a deeper reason neutrality matters, and it touches identity. Many capable people confuse "I have a thought" with "I must act on this now". They are conscientious. They do not like dropping balls. Yet not every thought requires immediate action, and treating all thoughts as urgent creates a life of permanent interruption. A neutral brain dump creates a gap between impulse and commitment. The gap is not laziness. It is discernment. The visible behaviour is a reduction in compulsive checking. When thoughts are reliably captured, the mind stops shouting. When the mind stops shouting, you can distinguish between true urgency and mental noise with more precision.

The counter-example is worth facing honestly, because the brain dump is not universally soothing. For some people, writing down concerns can temporarily increase their salience. It can make the mind feel more crowded, not less, especially if the capture turns into rumination or if the list becomes a catalogue of inadequacy. The reconciliation lies in the distinction between capture and evaluation. Expressive writing, of the kind Pennebaker studied, can be a deeper emotional practice with its own aims and effects. A fast brain dump is logistical. It is not asking you to interpret your life. It is asking you to record inputs neutrally so they can be handled in a deliberate sequence later. When a brain dump becomes a place to brood, it stops being a scratchpad and becomes a mirror, and mirrors are rarely helpful when the goal is to reduce noise quickly.

Another limitation is contextual. Some thoughts cannot be "captured and moved on" because they are ethical, relational, or existential in nature. A difficult conversation, a worry about a loved one, a professional dilemma that involves judgement and values. Reducing such concerns to a single line can feel disrespectful or inadequate. Yet even here, capture can still serve a purpose: it can name the concern without attempting to resolve it, which prevents the mind from repeatedly reconstructing it. Naming is not solving. Naming is containment. The mind often relaxes when it sees that a concern has been acknowledged and placed somewhere it will not be forgotten. The alternative is the endless replay that masquerades as responsibility while rarely producing a better outcome.

The practical power of a fast brain dump is therefore best understood as a change in how attention is allocated. Attention is not simply taken by what is important; it is taken by what is unresolved and uncontained. When you create a reliable scratchpad habit, you reduce the number of unresolved items that must be carried internally. That reduction has consequences across the week. The person becomes less reactive to incoming messages because they trust their ability to capture and decide later. They become less prone to late-night mental rehearsals because they know the thought has a home. They become less tempted to build ever more elaborate systems because the simplest system, used consistently, is now doing its job.

There is also a subtle form of dignity in fast capture. It refuses the melodrama of being "overwhelmed" while acknowledging the reality of being full. A life can be full without being broken. The brain dump is a small gesture of respect towards your own cognition: it admits that the mind is not a filing cabinet, and it stops punishing the mind for behaving like a mind. It replaces internal monitoring with external storage. It replaces repeated pings with a queue.

The scratchpad motif returns at the end because it points to the unresolved tension that makes this practice either transformative or useless. A scratchpad only works if it is trusted enough that you stop carrying a duplicate copy in your head. That trust is built through retrieval and follow-through, not through beautiful formatting. When you next feel the familiar ping while you are doing something else, the test is not whether you can ignore it. The test is whether you can capture it neutrally, in one trusted place, and then return to what you were doing without the itch to keep checking.

Chapter 4
A weekly review that fits

A person sits down with the best of intentions and opens their calendar to last week. It looks familiar and yet slightly alien, like a photograph taken from an angle they did not choose. There are blocks that were meant to contain work but leaked into the evening. There are commitments that happened and left no trace except tiredness. There are gaps that were supposed to be restful and became filled with errands, messages, and the small admin that never makes it onto the calendar because it is "too small to count". The person scrolls, and with each day the mind supplies a private commentary: should have, could have, why did I not. The review becomes a self-critique, and the impulse is to shut the laptop and walk away.

Another person avoids the calendar altogether. They look forward only. They tell themselves the past is unhelpful, that what matters is next week, that analysis is indulgent. They plan with determination and optimism, and then repeat the same pattern: a Tuesday that is always tight becomes tight again; a recurring delay point appears again; a task that always slips slips again. They are not blind. They simply have no structured way to notice what reality keeps insisting on. Without a review, the week becomes a series of fresh surprises that are not actually surprises.

The paradox is sharp: the weekly review is the part people most need and most resist. It feels like extra work and, more threateningly, it feels like a verdict. Yet without it, the mind never gets closure, and without closure the mind keeps monitoring and pinging. A review that fits is not a post-mortem and not a performance. It is a short, honest look at what happened so that the next set of decisions can be made with fewer fantasies and fewer repeated mistakes. The point is not to become a better person. The point is to stop losing time to patterns you have not named.

The tension here is between accuracy and self-protection. Look back too harshly and the review becomes punishing, which makes it unsustainable. Look back too softly and the review becomes vague, which makes it useless. The middle path requires a particular kind of emotional discipline: the ability to treat the past week as data without pretending that data is cold. Weeks are lived, not logged. They contain messy human factors: fatigue, interruptions, relationships, misjudgements, and the ordinary fact that time feels different at 9am than it does at 9pm. A review that fits does not deny any of this. It simply refuses to make it a courtroom.

This matters because planning without review is not merely inefficient; it is fragile. Fragility shows up as constant re-planning, the sense of always catching up, the feeling that the week is happening to you rather than being navigated by you. When you do not look back, you do not learn where your plans consistently collide with reality. You keep making promises to an imaginary version of yourself with unlimited energy and no interruptions. Reality then breaks those promises, and the mind responds by adding more monitoring: more checking, more worrying, more last-minute improvisation. The cost is not only time. The cost is trust in your own system.

It also matters because a review creates momentum in a way that no amount of future planning can. Momentum is not motivation. It is the quiet psychological effect of reducing open loops. When a few easy loops are closed while they are visible, the mental environment changes. The brain receives evidence that things do not have to remain pending. That evidence reduces noise. It also improves judgement, because decisions made in a clearer mental environment are less reactive. A review that includes small, bounded completions therefore does not merely tidy the past; it changes the quality of attention available for the week ahead.

A further stake is hidden in the phrase "waiting for". Many delays in adult life do not come from our own inaction but from dependence on other people and systems: someone else's reply, a document promised, a service to be delivered, a decision pending, a form processed. When these dependencies are not tracked, the mind repeatedly revisits them as vague concerns. It wonders whether to follow up, worries about being too pushy, forgets, remembers again, and burns attention in cycles. A lightweight way to hold these items turns circular worry into a clear prompt. It reduces the need to rethink the same uncertainty. It makes the week feel less like a haze of "I am waiting for something" and more like a set of known dependencies that can be checked at the right time.

The motif running through this chapter is the rear-view mirror. A driver does not stare into it, but a driver who never checks it is not brave, merely unaware. The mirror is glanced at briefly to reduce surprises, to see what is approaching, to understand positioning. A weekly review has the same purpose. It is a glance, not a dwelling. It does not exist to make you relive the week. It exists to prevent the week from blindsiding you with the same patterns again.

The path here begins with a quick scan of the week just lived, not to judge it, but to notice its shape and its friction points. It then turns to the small loops that can be closed quickly and cleanly while they are in view, without pretending that everything can be finished inside the reset hour. It ends with a simple way to hold the items that are not in your hands, so that dependence stops living as a repeated mental loop and becomes a trackable state. Each step is designed to be brief enough to be repeatable and honest enough to be useful.

The question that pulls us into the practical work is not whether last week was good or bad. The question is where it was *predictable*, and whether you have been treating that predictability as a personal failing rather than as information you can use. What, if you looked back without flinching, would you see repeating?

Scanning the past week

In Tokyo in July 1950, W. Edwards Deming delivered a series of lectures that would later be credited with helping Japanese industry rebuild its approach to quality by insisting on a disciplined relationship between observation and improvement (Deming, 1986). The practical idea was unromantic: do the work, then *check* what actually happened, then adjust. Not guess. Not moralise. Check. Deming was speaking to engineers and managers, but the underlying move applies to any life that wants to feel less like improvisation. If the past is not scanned, the future is planned from imagination.

The week leaves a trail. Meetings attended. Promises made. Tasks half-finished. Friction points repeated with weary consistency. Yet many people treat the week as something to survive rather than something to read. They carry the residue forward without looking at it directly, then wonder why the same bottlenecks reappear. A Tuesday that always tightens the schedule becomes tight again. A particular kind of admin always slips to the edge of the evening. A recurring obligation keeps arriving as a surprise despite having arrived before. The surprise is not the event. The surprise is the lack of an honest glance.

Scanning is not confession. It is measurement. A scan is brief, neutral, and oriented towards reality rather than self-image. The distinction matters because the weekly review is often resisted for the wrong reason. People imagine it as a tribunal: a session where failures are tallied and shortcomings exposed. That fantasy makes the scan emotionally dangerous, which encourages avoidance, which keeps the week unexamined, which ensures the next plan repeats the same errors. A scan that fits is closer to a scientist's field notes than a memoir. It is not intimate. It is useful.

A small scene shows how quickly the mind turns a scan into a story. Someone opens their calendar and sees the gap on Wednesday that was meant for focused work and became swallowed by interruptions. The instant reaction is not curiosity; it is judgement. They hear an internal voice that says they should have protected the time, should have said no, should have been more disciplined. None of this produces clarity. It produces shame, which is a powerful way to make the past feel dangerous. The alternative is not denial. It is a different question: what actually happened in that gap, and what does that reveal about how the week behaves? Naming the phenomenon changes its emotional temperature. Judgement burns. Noticing cools.

The concept underneath is calibration. Planning is only as good as its calibration to real constraints: how long tasks actually take, where interruptions reliably occur, which days carry hidden commitments, which transitions are always longer than expected. Without calibration, planning becomes a form of wishful thinking, and wishful thinking is fragile. It breaks under ordinary pressure. When it breaks, the mind compensates with monitoring and urgency, then calls the resulting stress "being busy". A scan is the calibration step. It updates the model of your week using evidence.

This is why the scan focuses on three kinds of data: what happened, what slipped, what surprised. "What happened" protects against selective memory, the tendency to remember only the loudest moments. The calendar is a blunt witness. "What slipped" identifies the recurring leak points where intentions fail to become actions, often because the next action was unclear or the timing was unrealistic. "What surprised" identifies where the plan lacked buffers, where someone else's dependency arrived without warning, or where a predictable energy dip was ignored. None of these categories requires self-punishment. They require attention to sequence. They are less about blame and more about pattern recognition.

One reason scanning is so hard is that memory does not behave like a recording. It behaves like a reconstruction. People do not simply retrieve last week; they rebuild it, and the rebuilding is biased by mood, fatigue, and the emotional charge of certain events. Hindsight bias is a well-studied example: once we know how something turned out, we tend to overestimate how predictable it was beforehand (Fischhoff, 1975). In weekly life this appears as the sentence, "I should have seen that coming," said about interruptions that were not, in fact, clearly foreseeable. The scan counters this bias by anchoring to traces: calendar entries, messages sent, notes captured. It moves the review from self-accusation towards evidence.

A second bias complicates scanning in a different way. When a week feels stressful, the mind tends to treat the most salient events as representative, which can distort planning. Tversky and Kahneman described how people rely on heuristics such as availability, where vivid examples come to mind easily and therefore feel more common than they are (Tversky and Kahneman, 1974). A single unpleasant meeting can colour the perception of the entire week. A single productive morning can generate unrealistic optimism about future capacity. The scan makes the week less vivid and more accurate. It asks, quietly, for distribution rather than drama: where did time and attention actually go?

This is where the rear-view mirror metaphor earns its keep, not as decoration but as a behavioural cue. A rear-view mirror is glanced at briefly and regularly, not stared into. Staring creates danger. Never glancing creates danger. The scan is that glance. It is short enough to avoid turning into rumination, structured enough to prevent the mind from cherry-picking, and honest enough to update your expectations for the week ahead. The crucial skill is to hold the mirror at the right angle: aimed at patterns, not at personal worth.

A checkable example of why this kind of glance matters comes from contexts where debriefs are treated as normal rather than as admissions of failure. After Apollo 11 in July 1969, NASA conducted post-mission analyses and debriefs to document anomalies, procedures, and lessons learned, not because the mission failed, but because complex work produces information even when it succeeds. The point is not to import NASA's formality into domestic life. The point is that scanning the past is not a punishment reserved for disasters. It is maintenance for systems that want to stay reliable. A week that "went fine" still contains data about what nearly slipped, what required last-minute improvisation, and what consumed more attention than expected. That data is valuable precisely because it is ordinary.

The scan also protects against a particular trap for high-functioning people: mistaking endurance for effectiveness. Someone can push through a week, meet deadlines, answer messages, keep the household running, and still have lived in constant reactive mode. If the scan is skipped, the only conclusion drawn is, "I survived, therefore the system works." Survival is not a high bar. A scan asks a more incisive question: what did survival cost, and which costs were avoidable? The avoidable costs are usually found in small repeatable friction points: transitions underestimated, commitments overstacked, "quick tasks" that were not runnable, dependencies untracked. Seeing those points turns stress into information.

There is, of course, a limitation. Scanning can become a subtle form of self-harm if it collapses into perfectionism, where every deviation is treated as evidence of failure and every surprise is treated as personal incompetence. Some people are especially prone to this because their standards are high and their identity is tied to competence. For them, review can feel like standing under a cold light. The reconciliation is to tighten the definition of the scan so it stays logistical. A scan is not an audit of character. It is a check on fit. Did the plan fit the week that actually existed? If not, where did it pinch? The language of "fit" is deliberately gentle and technical. A shoe that pinches is not a moral failing. It is a bad fit.

Another limitation is that not all weeks offer clean data. Illness, emergencies, and unpredictable care demands can shatter any plan. In such weeks, scanning for "what I could have done better" can be both inaccurate and cruel. Yet even here, a scan can serve a different purpose: to separate what was in your control from what was not, and to notice what protective buffers might be needed next time. The scan is not required to produce improvement every week. It is required to prevent fantasy from becoming the default planning method.

When scanning is done well, its outcomes are visible in the next set of decisions without needing to be announced. Tuesdays that are always tight stop being treated as empty canvases and start being treated as constrained days. A recurring late-afternoon energy dip stops being treated as laziness and starts being treated as a predictable condition. A meeting that always overruns stops being scheduled back-to-back with something fragile. These are not dramatic changes. They are calibrations. Calibration is what reduces the need for constant re-planning, which is one of the most exhausting forms of modern admin.

The rear-view mirror appears again at the point where many people go wrong. They either refuse to look back, then are surprised by what is behind them, or they look back too long and lose the ability to move forward. The scan is an instrument, not a dwelling. Its value is proportional to its brevity and its honesty. It should leave you with a clearer sense of the week's actual shape, not a thicker layer of self-commentary.

The forward tension is not whether scanning is wise. It is whether you can tolerate a week seen clearly. If the calendar showed you, without excuses or drama, the one day that always collapses under unrealistic planning, would you change your future expectations, or would you keep planning for a week that exists mainly in hope?

Closing small loops

In Amsterdam in 1632, Rembrandt painted *The Anatomy Lesson of Dr Nicolaes Tulp*, a composition that has survived not because it is tidy but because it is decisive: a group gathered around a single act of attention, a lesson made visible through focus (Rembrandt, 1632). The painting is not about productivity. Yet it offers a useful contrast to the way most people try to deal with life admin. They spread attention thin, touching many things without finishing any, as if breadth itself could substitute for closure. The result is not mastery. It is mental noise.

Closure changes the atmosphere.

Small loops are not grand responsibilities. They are the minor, persistent open ends that keep resurfacing: a message that needs a reply, a form that needs one missing detail, an appointment that must be confirmed or cancelled, a document that should be filed, a quick follow-up that keeps being postponed because it feels slightly awkward. Their power comes from their incompletion. A small open loop is like a low-level alarm that never stops ringing because the system cannot decide whether it is safe. The sound is often internal, not literal: a recurring thought, a subtle dread when opening an inbox, a feeling of "I should" that appears while doing something else. Left open, these loops do not simply wait. They interfere.

The instinctive response is to attack the list aggressively, as if completion were a moral purge. That approach rarely works inside a weekly reset, because the hour has limits. When people try to close everything, they either overrun, which makes the ritual unsustainable, or they stop with a sense of failure that discourages returning. The central tension is therefore between breadth and finish. The reset hour needs enough closure to quiet the mind, but not so much ambition that it becomes a punishing session. The solution is not willpower. It is selection: choosing which loops are small enough to close cleanly within the time you have.

A concrete scene shows what "small" really means. Someone opens their capture inbox and sees a dozen items. One is a missed RSVP. Another is a note to reorder something. Another is "send the document". Another is "call about the bill". The mind flinches because these items are not equal in complexity, and yet they sit side by side like identical weights. The person begins to dabble, opening one, realising it requires information, switching to another, starting a draft, then getting distracted by a new message. The hour becomes a swirl. This is the failure mode of unselected loops: attention is distributed across too many partly opened tasks. The concept here is completion as attention management, not as virtue. The implication is that a few clean closures can do more to reduce mental noise than a hundred half-starts.

Psychology has language for why completion feels so disproportionately relieving. The Zeigarnik effect, first described by Bluma Zeigarnik in 1927, suggests that unfinished tasks can remain more salient in memory than finished ones (Zeigarnik, 1927). Later work has complicated the picture, but the everyday phenomenon is familiar: unresolved items keep returning. More recent research points to the role of plans and commitment in reducing intrusive goal-related thoughts; Masicampo and Baumeister reported that forming a plan could reduce such intrusions (Masicampo and Baumeister, 2011). The implication for weekly review is practical. A loop quietens when it is genuinely closed or when its next state is made stable. Stability is what the mind craves, because stability reduces the need for monitoring.

To close a loop, then, is to create a state change that the brain can trust. Sometimes that state change is finishing. Sometimes it is delegating, which is not merely "asking someone" but transferring ownership clearly enough that you no longer need to rehearse it internally. Sometimes it is deleting, which is not nihilism but clarity: deciding that a task does not matter, or does not matter now, and releasing it rather than letting it masquerade as a pending obligation. Deleting is often the most emotionally difficult closure because it requires admitting that you cannot do everything and that some commitments were never true commitments. Yet deletion can be a relief precisely because it removes a false loop: a thing you have been carrying out of guilt rather than intention.

The phrase "within the hour" is the discipline that prevents loop-closing from becoming another performance. The hour is a container. Containers require boundaries. When people ignore the container, they start closing loops in a way that is not sustainable: chasing deeper issues, pursuing perfection, handling tasks that are small in name but large in hidden steps. This is where the earlier discussion of "tiny tasks" returns as a warning. A loop that looks small can turn into a twenty-minute detour if it lacks a key detail. A loop that is socially charged can expand because it triggers rumination. A loop that requires a decision can stall because the decision is uncomfortable. The implication is that small-loop closure is not about courage. It is about choosing the loops whose closure is likely, not merely desirable.

A checkable example from outside personal life shows why organisations prioritise closing small loops rather than endlessly reopening them. In software development, teams often track bugs and minor issues in a backlog. A team that never closes small bugs creates a product that feels unreliable, not because any one bug is catastrophic, but because the cumulative friction erodes trust. The best teams distinguish between work that requires a project and work that can be resolved quickly, because quick resolutions reduce noise in the system. They also delete or deprioritise items that do not matter, because a backlog that includes everything becomes meaningless. The personal analogue is direct. A task list that includes every half-thought becomes a catalogue of guilt. A weekly review that closes a few small loops turns the list back into a tool.

The experience of momentum is often misunderstood as motivation, as if certain people simply have more drive. In practice, momentum is frequently produced by reduced cognitive load. When a few loops are closed, the mind has fewer items to monitor. With fewer items to monitor, attention becomes less fragmented. With less fragmentation, it becomes easier to complete other tasks. This is not a mystical upward spiral. It is a change in conditions. You can observe it in the body: fewer glances at the phone, fewer aimless app switches, less restless reopening of the same inbox thread. Momentum is an emergent property of closure.

Yet there is an important limitation to address, because "closing small loops" can become a way of avoiding the work that truly matters. People can spend an hour clearing minor items and feel productive while the larger projects that require sustained attention remain untouched. This is the classic trap of the urgent and the easy. It is also a trap of comfort. Small loops are often easier because they have clear endpoints and quick rewards, while larger work is ambiguous and demanding. The reconciliation is to keep the purpose of small-loop closure in view. The weekly review is not a place to complete everything; it is a place to reduce mental noise and to create a workable plan for what matters. Small loops earn their place when they reduce friction and release attention, not when they serve as a convenient substitute for deeper commitments.

This is why the "easiest" loops are not necessarily the smallest in time, but the smallest in ambiguity. A loop is easy when you know exactly what to do, have what you need to do it, and can complete it without opening additional questions. A loop is hard when it requires searching for information, making a value-laden decision, or coordinating with someone else. Hard loops may still need progress, but they may not belong in the closure phase of the weekly review. They may belong in the parking list or in a scheduled block. The implication is that wise closure is not about clearing the maximum number of items. It is about clearing the right kind of items to change the mental environment of the week.

The motif to hold onto is the knot. A small loop is a loose knot in the week: not dramatic, but snagging. When you close a few knots, movement becomes smoother. When you tug at every knot at once, you tighten the tangle. Closing small loops is the act of choosing which knots can be undone cleanly with the time and attention available, so the week stops catching on them.

A final, quieter reason small-loop closure matters is social. Many small loops involve other people: replies owed, confirmations needed, follow-ups promised. Leaving them open creates a subtle drag on relationships and professional credibility. It also creates internal discomfort because social obligations are particularly sticky in memory; they are tied to identity and reciprocity. Closing a few of these loops can therefore produce disproportionate relief. Not because social life is a ledger, but because unresolved social commitments keep the mind rehearsing.

The forward test is not whether you could close more loops if you tried harder. It is whether you can choose closure that actually reduces monitoring. When you look at your open loops, which ones, if closed, would make the week feel quieter within minutes, and which ones are you tempted to "close" only because they are easier than facing what truly requires a longer block of attention?

Updating your "waiting for" list

On 27 March 1977 at Los Rodeos Airport in Tenerife, a foggy runway became the setting for a tragedy shaped not only by speed and metal, but by something quieter: uncertainty about clearance, position, and who was waiting for whom. KLM Flight 4805 began its take-off roll while Pan Am Flight 1736 was still on the runway, and a chain of miscommunication and assumptions ended in disaster. Aviation investigators and historians have returned to this event for decades because it reveals an uncomfortable truth: in complex systems, waiting is not passive. Waiting is a state that must be named and managed, or it turns into guesswork, and guesswork invites failure.

Waiting has its own cost.

Most lives are not airfields. Yet the same dynamic plays out in smaller, more personal ways every week. A person sends a message asking for a document and then half-remembers it during unrelated tasks. They request a repair and then keep an ear tuned for the doorbell. They submit a form and then repeatedly check for updates because they cannot bear the possibility that something has gone wrong unnoticed. The mind does not experience this as "waiting". It experiences it as low-level vigilance, a constant readiness to pounce when the awaited thing arrives, coupled with the fear that it will not arrive at all.

The hidden problem is that dependence creates open loops that feel different from self-assigned tasks. When the next step belongs to someone else or to a system, personal effort cannot directly close the loop. The result is a peculiar cognitive itch. People keep revisiting the same concern not because they are impatient, but because the status is unclear and the consequences of missing it can be socially costly: a delayed project, an awkward apology, a missed appointment, a promise broken by accident rather than intent. In practical terms, dependence turns the mind into a monitoring device. It keeps asking, "Has it happened yet?" and because the answer is often "I do not know", it asks again.

This is where a "waiting for" list earns its place as a deceptively powerful tool. It is not a complicated system. It is a deliberate acknowledgement that some of the week's most stressful loose ends are not tasks in the usual sense. They are dependencies. A dependency is an item whose next action is not "do the thing" but "notice whether the thing arrives, and if not, follow up at the right moment". Without a container for dependencies, the mind tries to manage them by periodic recall, which is both unreliable and exhausting. The "waiting for" list replaces recall with a record. That record changes behaviour: the person checks the list at a chosen time rather than being yanked into rethinking by random pings.

A small scene shows how dependence turns into drift. A person has asked a colleague for a specific dataset or a short approval. They cannot proceed without it. They send the message on Monday. On Tuesday they wonder if it has been seen. On Wednesday they feel awkward following up. On Thursday they start building a workaround that wastes time. On Friday they receive the dataset, and the week ends with a rush of late work that could have been steadier if the dependency had been tracked and nudged at the right point. This is not a story about blame. It is a story about information. When dependencies are untracked, the mind oscillates between passivity and panic, and both are costly. The concept is dependency visibility. The implication is simple: what is visible can be managed; what is vague becomes mental noise.

The mind's tendency to revisit unclosed loops has been discussed earlier, but dependencies add a twist. You cannot complete a loop that is not in your hands, so the mind seeks relief in rechecking instead. This aligns with research suggesting that unfinished goals can generate intrusive thoughts and that forming plans can reduce those intrusions

(Masicampo and Baumeister, 2011). A "waiting for" list is not a plan in the grand sense, yet it does something similar. It answers the brain's question about what happens next. It says: this is pending, and there is a defined point at which it will be checked or chased. That defined point matters. It reduces the urge to keep the item warm in working memory.

A second checkable example, from a domain where dependencies are treated as engineering problems, makes the logic more vivid. In April 1970, during Apollo 13, mission teams had to operate with extreme constraints and a constant stream of dependencies: power budgets, life-support parameters, communications windows, and the need for specific calculations and hardware procedures to arrive on time. The striking feature of Mission Control was not simply competence; it was explicit tracking. Unknowns were named. Responsibilities were assigned. Follow-ups were scheduled. Waiting existed, but it was not allowed to remain amorphous. The implication for ordinary life is not to cosplay as an astronaut. It is to notice that when stakes are high, people stop relying on memory to manage dependencies. They externalise.

In everyday life, dependencies are everywhere and often socially delicate. A person is waiting for a school response, a medical appointment confirmation, a bank letter, a delivery update, a friend's reply, a contractor's quote, a colleague's feedback, an administrator's processing time. Each item carries a different kind of uncertainty: some are time-bound, others are "whenever". Some are likely to arrive quickly, others are notorious for delay. When these items are not tracked, the mind creates its own informal tracking system: checking the inbox repeatedly, opening the same chat thread, scanning notifications, revisiting the thought while walking to the shop. This is the behaviour you can measure without numbers: how often you check, how often you re-open, how often you mentally rehearse follow-up messages. The "waiting for" list reduces these behaviours by giving them a place to land.

It also clarifies a crucial distinction between *patience* and *passivity*. Patience is chosen. Passivity is accidental. A person can choose to wait because a follow-up too soon would be unhelpful or because a system legitimately needs time. Passivity happens when the person does not quite know when to check again, so they drift. Drift is stressful because it combines the worst of both worlds: the work is not progressing, yet the mind is still expending effort. A "waiting for" list transforms drift into a defined state. It turns "I am vaguely waiting for something" into "this item is pending, and the next check occurs at a chosen moment". That is control without pretence.

The list is also a quiet defence against a specific kind of friction: social guilt. Many people avoid following up because they fear being annoying, or because they have internalised a rule that needing something is an imposition. This fear does not remove the dependency. It simply pushes it into the shadows, where it continues to create stress while progress stalls. Tracking dependencies does not make a person more demanding; it makes them more honest about what their work and life require. The behavioural shift is subtle: follow-ups become less emotionally loaded because they are no longer reactive bursts of frustration. They become routine check-ins prompted by a system, rather than by impatience.

A well-kept "waiting for" list also reduces duplicate work, which is a common but under-recognised cost of unmanaged dependence. When a person is unsure whether something will arrive, they sometimes begin alternative paths "just in case": starting a different application, creating a workaround, redoing a task with partial information, assembling documents repeatedly. These workarounds can be prudent in some contexts, but they are often born from uncertainty rather than strategy. The list introduces a choice point. It forces the question: is this dependency likely to arrive in time, or does it require escalation or an alternative plan? Even when the answer is to wait, the waiting becomes explicit rather than anxious.

The quiet motif here is the receipt. When you hand something over at a counter, you are often given a receipt: proof that you requested something, a reference for follow-up, a way to avoid repeating the entire transaction from scratch. A "waiting for" list functions like a shelf of receipts. It holds evidence of what you have already asked for, when you asked, and what you expect back. The receipt does not speed up the process by itself. It reduces uncertainty. It stops you doubting your own memory. It gives you a stable reference when you do need to follow up. Without a receipt, people re-explain and re-request, which is tiring and can irritate others. With a receipt, the follow-up is cleaner.

Of course, there is a limitation worth stating plainly. Not all waiting is trackable in a satisfying way. Some systems are opaque. Some people are unreliable. Some outcomes are genuinely uncertain. A list cannot force a reply. A list cannot guarantee a processing time. A list cannot prevent a disappointment. If treated as a magical device, it will fail and increase frustration. The reconciliation is to redefine what success looks like. The purpose of the "waiting for" list is not to control other people. It is to control your attention. It aims to reduce the repeated rethinking that turns dependency into background stress. Even when a dependency remains unresolved, a tracked dependency is less mentally corrosive than an untracked one, because it has a defined place and a defined next check.

There is another limitation that thoughtful people should take seriously: overtracking can become a form of anxiety. If a person adds every trivial dependency to the list and then checks it compulsively, the list becomes another monitoring device rather than a relief. The list should reduce checking, not institutionalise it. This is where the weekly review context matters. The "waiting for" list is refreshed and consulted at chosen moments, not endlessly throughout the day. Its power comes from periodic attention, not constant attention. In other words, the receipt shelf is useful because you do not stand at the counter staring at it. You glance when needed, then continue living.

A "waiting for" list also clarifies responsibility, which is often where stress hides. Some items are genuinely out of your hands. Others feel out of your hands because you have not named the next action clearly. For example, "waiting for appointment confirmation" might actually mean "I need to choose a time window and send availability". "Waiting for the contractor" might actually mean "I need to send the photos and measurements they requested". The list does not only track other people; it reveals where you have mistaken your own next step for someone else's. That revelation reduces self-deception, which is a surprisingly large part of life admin.

The implications ripple across the week. When dependencies are tracked, a person becomes less prone to last-minute panic because they can see what is pending. They can also see what is *not* pending, which matters just as much. Many people spend mental energy worrying about whether they asked for something, whether they replied, whether they sent the document. A simple record turns those worries into a checkable fact. The mind relaxes when facts replace suspense. Trust increases. The system feels more dependable, and dependability is what makes the Sunday reset sustainable.

The receipt motif returns in one final way. A receipt is not a guarantee. It is a claim ticket. It allows you to say, calmly and clearly, "This is what I requested, and this is what I am still owed." That clarity can protect professional relationships and personal ones alike, because it reduces the emotional charge of follow-up. It also protects your own sense of competence. You stop relying on hazy recollection. You can point to the record. You can act from it.

The forward test is therefore a question about attention rather than administration. When you are waiting on something that matters, do you carry it as an internal loop, rethinking it in scattered moments, or do you give it a receipt and a place to live so that your mind can stop patrolling for what is missing?

Chapter 5
Choosing next-week priorities

A person sits down on Sunday with the week ahead open in front of them and feels a familiar lurch. The list is long. The calendar is already crowded. Messages have arrived that carry an undertone of urgency, and the mind reacts the way it always does when it senses demand outstripping capacity: it starts to grab. It grabs the loud tasks first, the ones that feel most pressing, the ones that come with social discomfort if ignored. The plan begins as triage. It becomes a scramble. By the end, the person has not chosen priorities so much as yielded to pressure.

Another person responds with the opposite reflex. They refuse to look closely. They make a few optimistic notes, reassure themselves that they will "just get on with it", and close the laptop quickly, as if attention itself might summon trouble. Monday arrives, and the week chooses for them. The urgent expands to fill the available space, important work is pushed into evenings and then postponed, and by Thursday a quiet dread has returned: the sense of being busy without being directed. The problem is not effort. It is selection.

Selection hurts.

That is the central tension of this chapter. Choosing priorities is not a mere organisational step; it is a confrontation with limits. It requires admitting that not everything will be done, and that some things will be delayed not by accident but by decision. Many people avoid this confrontation by creating long lists that include everything, which feels honest but is often a form of emotional avoidance: if everything is listed, no painful choice has been made. The cost of avoiding the choice arrives later as guilt and constant mental monitoring. A week without priorities is not a neutral week. It is a week governed by whatever pings loudest.

The stakes are not only personal comfort. Priority decisions determine which promises are kept, which relationships are honoured, and which forms of work receive the best attention rather than the leftovers. When priorities are unclear, the mind stays in a state of readiness, scanning for threats. That scanning produces the feeling of being "on", even during rest, because the brain is trying to prevent a miss. When priorities are clear, attention can narrow and deepen. Deep attention improves quality. It also reduces waste, because fewer hours are spent rethinking and rechecking. A priority is, in effect, a permission structure: it tells the mind what deserves protection and what can safely wait.

This chapter also continues a theme running through the entire reset: the difference between control and performance. Performance planning looks impressive. It produces packed schedules and ambitious task lists. It feels like competence. Control planning is less flattering. It makes hard commitments visible, accepts energy limits, and creates a short list that can actually be finished. It does not pretend that big projects will fit into small gaps. It creates a place for them that is honest. The trade-off is emotional. Performance satisfies the part of the mind that wants to feel capable. Control satisfies the part of the mind that wants to be able to trust what it has promised.

A subtle danger appears here, and it is worth naming early. When people say "urgent", they often mean "uncomfortable". Social discomfort is a powerful motivator. An unanswered message can feel urgent not because something will break, but because silence feels rude. A bureaucratic task can feel urgent not because the deadline is near, but because the paperwork is irritating. The mind tends to confuse emotional pressure with temporal constraint. This confusion turns the Sunday reset into a panic session: a flurry of reaction rather than a deliberate choice. The antidote is not calmness as a personality trait. It is a test that separates external deadlines from internal noise, so urgency is treated as a fact rather than as a feeling.

The long-term stakes are even more revealing. A week planned without priorities often produces a particular kind of regret: not regret about being lazy, but regret about misallocation. The person did things. They were busy. They might even have been helpful. Yet the outcomes that would have made the week feel meaningful did not happen, because they were never named clearly enough to defend against interruption. This is where "outcomes" matter. Outcomes are not vague aspirations. They are the few concrete results that, if achieved, would change how the week feels in retrospect. Without them, tasks become a blur. With them, tasks become subordinate to something that can be recognised as progress. Recognition matters. It is how the mind learns that effort is producing value rather than merely motion.

The motif for this chapter is the tray. Not the inbox tray from capture, but a serving tray: the limited surface that forces selection. A tray cannot hold everything in the kitchen. It holds what will be carried into the next room. When people try to carry everything, they drop things. When they carry nothing deliberate, they make repeated trips. A good weekly plan is a tray. It carries a small number of chosen outcomes and a realistic shortlist of actions, while the rest is either safely delayed or placed somewhere that will be handled properly later. The tray is not a sign of scarcity. It is a sign of respect for gravity.

The path here moves from the pressure of urgency to the clarity of what truly breaks if it waits, then to the discipline of naming a few outcomes that define success in concrete terms, then to the construction of a shortlist that matches real time and energy rather than imagined capacity. It also requires a final act of honesty: recognising which longer projects are being smuggled into the week as vague intentions, and giving them a proper container rather than pretending they will happen in the margins. The sequence is not about productivity as a moral pursuit. It is about making the week runnable.

The unresolved friction that pulls us into the work is this: when you look at the week ahead, which items feel urgent because they have real deadlines, and which feel urgent because they make you uncomfortable to ignore?

Separating urgent and important

In June 1944 at Southwick House in Hampshire, Dwight D. Eisenhower faced a kind of pressure that strips language down to essentials. Weather, timing, logistics, and human lives were braided together so tightly that a single decision would ripple across everything that followed. The situation produced urgent signals in abundance: forecasts shifting, messages arriving, plans that needed confirmation, contingencies that threatened to sprawl. Yet the most decisive work was not the frantic handling of every signal. It was the ability to discriminate between what demanded immediate movement and what demanded sober protection. Urgency was loud. Importance was quieter.

Noise is persuasive.

That is why the urgent so often steals the week. In ordinary life, urgency rarely arrives as a clear deadline stamped on a document. It arrives as a feeling in the chest when the phone lights up. It arrives as a subject line that looks sharp. It arrives as the discomfort of leaving someone waiting. It arrives as the dread of a form you do not want to face. The mind, designed to respond quickly to potential threats, treats these signals as if they were equal in consequence. They are not. A weekly reset becomes a panic session precisely when feelings of pressure are mistaken for facts of timing.

A useful definition is surprisingly plain. Urgent means time-sensitive in a way that carries an external consequence if missed. Important means consequential in a way that improves or protects life, work, or relationships even when no immediate deadline is visible. These categories are not moral labels; they are descriptive. The trouble starts when urgent is defined by *emotional heat* rather than by an external constraint. Emotional heat is real, but it is not a reliable scheduling tool. It is easily triggered by ambiguity, social discomfort, and the simple fact of unread messages. When emotional heat is treated as urgency, attention becomes reactive, and the week becomes a series of flinches.

The Sunday reset is where this flinch can be interrupted, because it offers a moment to compare sensation with reality. The comparison is the work. It looks, at first glance, like a minor semantic distinction, but it changes behaviour in concrete ways: what gets scheduled, what gets deferred without guilt, what receives the best attention rather than the scraps. "Efficiency" becomes fewer interruptions rather than faster typing. "Risk" becomes a clear view of what would genuinely fail if delayed, rather than a vague fear that everything will unravel. "Trust" becomes the quiet confidence that you have not merely reacted to the loudest inputs, but chosen deliberately.

The simplest test for this comparison is almost impolite in its bluntness: what breaks if this waits a week? The power of the question is that it forces a concrete answer. If the answer is "an appointment is missed", "a deadline is breached", "someone cannot proceed without my input", or "a fee is incurred", the urgency is anchored in the world. If the answer is "I will feel uneasy", "I do not like leaving it", or "I will keep thinking about it", the urgency is likely psychological rather than temporal. Psychological urgency matters, but it is a different category. It is often an open loop craving closure rather than a true time constraint. Naming the difference reduces panic because it prevents the mind from treating discomfort as an emergency.

This is not merely philosophy. It is a description of how attention behaves under uncertainty. Daniel Kahneman has written about how the mind relies on fast, intuitive judgements when under cognitive strain, prioritising what is salient, immediate, and emotionally charged (Kahneman, 2011). Urgent-looking items tend to be salient. They flash. They interrupt. They demand. Important items often do none of this. They are quieter and more structural: preventive care, long-term projects, thoughtful conversations, maintenance, preparation. Salience is not the same as significance. Yet without a deliberate sorting mechanism, salience tends to win, and the week fills with response rather than with intention.

A small scene makes the distinction painfully clear. A person sits down to plan the week and immediately opens the inbox, because that is where pressure is most visible. They see messages that can be replied to quickly and messages that cannot. They respond to the quick ones and feel momentarily lighter. They then notice a complex message that requires a decision and feel a jolt of discomfort. They postpone it. They scan again. More messages appear. The hour is consumed by reaction. The week ahead is still unshaped. In this pattern, urgency is not determined by consequences. It is determined by what is easiest to clear, what is socially awkward to ignore, and what is loudest. The implication is that the reset has been captured by *the siren*, the internal alarm that interprets immediate discomfort as the most important thing.

A second named, checkable moment shows how even in high-stakes settings the urgent can be a trap if it crowds out the important. In October 1962 in Washington, D.C., during the Cuban Missile Crisis, the Executive Committee of the National Security Council (ExComm) dealt with a flood of urgent inputs: intelligence updates, military options, diplomatic communications, time pressure. Historians have examined the period precisely because urgency was everywhere and yet the most consequential decisions required restraint, sequencing, and deliberate escalation management. The point is not to drag geopolitics into domestic planning. The point is that urgency is not automatically the same as wise action. Under pressure, systems that survive tend to create deliberative spaces where signal can be separated from noise. Your week deserves a smaller version of that space.

The decisive move is to treat "urgent" as a claim that must be tested, not a command that must be obeyed. Testing does not mean doubting your instincts in some abstract way. It means anchoring the sense of urgency in observable criteria: a fixed time, a dependency, a deadline, a hard commitment, a constraint that can be written down. If the urgency cannot be anchored, it belongs in a different category: either important but not urgent, or neither important nor urgent but psychologically sticky. Those sticky items are often the ones that create background stress, because they are unresolved. They want closure. Closure can be achieved by deciding, not necessarily by doing. This is why the question "what breaks if this waits a week?" is so potent: it distinguishes between "this must happen" and "this wants to stop bothering me".

Important work is often threatened by two forces: invisibility and substitution. Invisibility because it does not shout. Substitution because urgent tasks provide the satisfying feeling of being needed, while important tasks often require solitude, concentration, or uncomfortable decisions. People can spend a week being extremely useful and still feel vaguely dissatisfied, because usefulness was defined by responding rather than by building. Important work tends to be cumulative. It produces outcomes that alter the shape of life: relationships strengthened, health maintained, research advanced, systems improved, friction reduced. When it is postponed repeatedly, nothing breaks immediately. That is precisely why it is vulnerable. The consequence arrives later as fragility: the week becomes more reactive because the foundations were not maintained.

There is a further complication that thoughtful people will recognise: the urgent can be contagious. One urgent request often produces more urgent requests, because quick responsiveness trains others and trains your own nervous system. A person who replies instantly becomes the person others rely on for instant replies. A person who always rescues the last-minute crisis becomes part of the crisis machinery. This is not an accusation; it is a systems effect. Boundaries and deliberate prioritisation interrupt the contagion by shifting behaviour from immediate response to planned response. The metric is visible. Fewer last-minute scrambles. Fewer "can you do this now?" messages that become automatic yeses. More commitments that are accepted only after checking the calendar and the shortlist.

A credible limitation needs to be acknowledged, or the concept becomes smug. Some roles and seasons collapse the distinction between urgent and important because the work is inherently time-sensitive. Emergency medicine, frontline care, crisis response, certain operational roles, childcare moments, and acute family needs can make urgency the correct organising principle for a period. In such contexts, the aim is not to pretend urgency can be eliminated, but to prevent false urgency from stealing what little discretionary attention remains. Even in a week dominated by real urgency, some important work still exists in the margins: a key follow-up, a necessary handover, a short planning moment that prevents avoidable confusion. The reconciliation is to treat the urgent/important distinction not as an ideology but as a diagnostic tool: it clarifies where you have genuine constraints and where you have merely inherited anxiety.

The distinction also becomes messy when "urgent" is socially mediated. A colleague's impatience can mimic a deadline. A family member's tone can turn a request into a demand. A bureaucracy can use language that makes everything sound immediate. The mind, especially a conscientious one, interprets these cues as risk. The antidote is not cynicism. It is a return to consequences. What breaks if this waits a week? What breaks if this waits a day? What breaks if this waits until Tuesday? The question converts social pressure into a concrete trade-off, and trade-offs are the real material of adult planning. This does not remove discomfort. It prevents discomfort from masquerading as a schedule.

The siren motif returns because the problem is not that urgency exists. The problem is that urgency is often performed, and the mind mistakes performance for danger. A siren makes you look. It is supposed to. The skill is not to become numb to sirens, but to step back and identify whether this particular sound corresponds to a real emergency or to a noisy vehicle passing through. When the week is planned under the spell of sirens, important work is repeatedly pushed into the shadows, then paid for later with compounded stress. When the week is planned with a tested definition of urgency, important work can be protected because it has been named explicitly and given a place.

The unresolved tension at the end of this is not whether you understand the concept. It is whether you can tolerate the discomfort of not responding to every siren. When you face the week ahead, which items are truly urgent because something will break, and which are merely pressing because you dislike leaving them unanswered?

Defining three weekly outcomes

In Santa Clara, California, in 1983, Intel's chief executive Andy Grove published *High Output Management*, a book that treated managerial work as a discipline of clarity rather than charisma. Grove's world was not poetry and not therapy; it was factories, deadlines, coordination, and the quiet reality that effort without direction becomes expensive. One of the book's lasting contributions was its insistence on distinguishing activity from results: not what people did all day, but what their work produced. That distinction sounds obvious until you try to apply it to a crowded week, where motion is constant and meaning can feel oddly absent.

A week can be busy and still disappointing. The disappointment rarely comes from idleness. It comes from drift. A person can answer messages, attend meetings, handle errands, clear small admin, and still reach Friday with the unsettling sense that nothing important actually moved. The mind remembers the exertion, yet cannot point to a small set of finished realities that justify it. That gap between effort and outcome is where resentment grows, and where the Sunday reset can become either a panic session or a quiet act of authorship.

Make the week legible again.

The core move is to stop treating tasks as the unit of a successful week. Tasks are actions. Outcomes are states of the world that change because those actions happened. "Reply to dentist" is a task. "Appointment booked and attended" is an outcome. "Look at finances" is a task. "Bills checked and one decision made" is an outcome. Outcomes resist vagueness. They force a boundary around what "done" means, which is why they are so useful for time-conscious people whose weeks are otherwise shaped by interruption and social pressure. When outcomes are named, a week stops being a pile of obligations and starts becoming a sequence of intended results.

A scene from ordinary professional life makes the difference visible. Someone plans the week by listing tasks as they arrive: send the draft, chase the reply, fill in the form, schedule the call, buy the thing, answer the email. The list grows quickly and remains stubbornly flat: each item looks like a peer, no matter how important it is. By midweek, the person is prioritising by immediacy rather than consequence, because immediacy is what can be felt. The loud tasks win. The quiet work that would truly change the week is postponed because it does not shout. The concept is attentional allocation: what you name as success determines what your attention defends. The implication is blunt. If "success" is defined as "be responsive", the week will be responsive. If "success" is defined as "achieve a few concrete results", responsiveness becomes one tool among others rather than the whole identity.

Outcomes also protect against a specific cognitive trap: substitution. Substitution is when the mind replaces a hard question with an easier one without noticing. A hard question is, "What result would make this week meaningfully better?" An easier question is, "What can I tick off quickly?" The easier question is not stupid. It is soothing. It gives the nervous system fast relief. Yet the cost appears later as the familiar Friday feeling: a week spent in reaction. Defining a small number of outcomes blocks substitution by keeping the hard question visible. It creates a reference point against which tasks can be measured: does this action contribute to one of the chosen results, or is it merely loud?

The usefulness of outcomes is not a modern productivity fashion. It is an old method for reducing ambiguity. When John F. Kennedy spoke at Rice University in Houston on 12 September 1962, he framed the space programme not as a collection of tasks but as an outcome: landing a man on the Moon and returning him safely to the Earth. The sentence did not specify the thousand component actions. It did something more important. It defined success in a way that could guide decisions, resource allocation, and trade-offs under uncertainty. The point is not to inflate domestic life into a national programme. The point is that outcomes create coherence. They allow a complex system to choose among competing demands because the system has a clear destination.

A well-chosen outcome has three properties that make it psychologically potent. It is concrete enough to be recognised as complete. It is narrow enough to fit inside a week without becoming theatre. And it is consequential enough that completing it changes the texture of life, work, or relationships. That last property matters because it distinguishes outcomes from self-improvement slogans. "Get healthier" is not an outcome; it is an aspiration that invites guilt. "Book the dentist and attend" is an outcome because it is a specific state change with a clear end. The behaviour associated with concrete outcomes is also different. People stop rewriting their lists and start choosing the next action that makes the outcome more likely: making the call, finding the required document, scheduling the slot, arranging the travel time. The implication is practical. Outcomes turn attention into a sequence of decisions rather than a swirl of intentions.

This is where the "three" matters, not as superstition but as constraint. A week can hold many tasks, but it cannot hold endless *priorities* without collapsing into conflict. The human mind can keep a small number of high-level aims active without constant checking; beyond that, it starts to forget, substitute, and react. A limited set of outcomes acts like a filter. It reduces decision fatigue because the question "what should I do next?" becomes less open-ended. It also reduces guilt because the mind has a plausible definition of "enough": if the outcomes are achieved, the week can be judged as successful even if the task list is not empty. An empty list is a fantasy for most adult lives. A meaningful outcome set is not.

The headline motif helps here because it captures what outcomes really do. A task list is a log of activity. An outcome is more like a headline: a short statement that would make the week feel real in retrospect. Not a dramatic headline, not a performative one, simply a true one. "Appointment handled." "Draft delivered." "Family admin stabilised." "Conversation had." The headline test is quietly clarifying because it exposes vagueness. If the headline cannot be written without hand-waving, the outcome is not yet defined. If it can be written in plain language, it can guide choices. The mind likes headlines because they compress complexity into meaning without denying that the complexity exists.

A named, checkable example from organisational practice shows how outcomes can discipline action without requiring micromanagement. Intel's later popularisation of goal-setting frameworks associated with "objectives" and "key results" is often linked to Grove's era and thinking, and the core idea is consistent with what matters here: define what success looks like, then allow actions to be chosen and adjusted in service of it. Even if a person has never used formal frameworks, the underlying logic applies to a personal week. When the outcome is clear, you can tolerate flexibility in the tasks. When the outcome is vague, you compensate by overplanning tasks, because the only way to feel control is to specify actions in excessive detail. That is how planning becomes brittle and exhausting.

Still, outcomes have a limitation that must be taken seriously if this is to remain honest rather than doctrinaire. Some weeks contain work whose results cannot be guaranteed inside a seven-day window: research that depends on discovery, negotiations that depend on other people, caregiving situations that change daily, creative work that resists scheduling. For such weeks, outcome-setting can become either unrealistic or oppressive if it is interpreted as a promise rather than a direction. The reconciliation is to define outcomes that reflect what is genuinely controllable and recognisable without pretending to control the uncontrollable. "Submit the application" is controllable. "Get accepted" is not. "Have the conversation" is controllable. "Resolve the relationship issue" may not be. "Send the draft" is controllable. "Receive glowing feedback" is not. The point is not to shrink life. It is to choose outcomes that do not require fortune to count as success.

Another limitation is emotional. Outcomes can trigger perfectionism if they are chosen as a way to prove something about oneself, rather than as a way to guide attention. This is where the Sunday reset's broader standard matters: clear enough to move on, not perfect enough to impress. Outcomes should reduce monitoring, not create a new standard that forces constant self-evaluation. The behavioural metric is telling. If naming outcomes makes you check your list obsessively and feel perpetually behind, the outcomes have been chosen or interpreted in the wrong spirit. If naming outcomes reduces rechecking and increases a calm sense of direction, they are doing their job.

The headline motif returns at the point where the week becomes crowded. When the inbox fills and the calendar tightens, the mind will be tempted to abandon the outcomes and chase what shouts. That is the moment outcomes earn their keep. They do not remove urgency. They help you decide which urgent items deserve immediate action and which can wait because they do not truly break anything. They also make trade-offs visible. Trade-offs are unavoidable. Outcomes simply ensure that trade-offs are chosen rather than stumbled into.

The forward test is therefore not whether you can produce a clever set of goals. It is whether you can name a small number of week-headlines that would make you trust your own life more by Friday, and then tolerate everything else being secondary. Which three outcomes would change the story of the week, and which tasks are you clinging to only because they are loud enough to feel urgent?

Creating a realistic task shortlist

In 1911 in Philadelphia, Frederick Winslow Taylor published *The Principles of Scientific Management*, insisting that work could be studied, measured, and redesigned rather than merely endured. The book has been praised and criticised for more than a century, and rightly so, yet one of its enduring provocations still lands: productivity problems are often design problems. People fail not only because they are careless, but because the system asks the impossible. A task list can do the same. It can ask more than a human week can carry, then blame the human for dropping what never fit in the first place.

Overfull lists are common because they feel honest. They record reality as it arrives: requests, intentions, ideas, obligations, hopes, and guilt, all poured into one place. The mind experiences a brief relief when the items are written down, as if naming them were the same as handling them. Then the list is reopened on a Wednesday afternoon, and the relief curdles. The list looks like evidence of failure-in-progress. It is too long to be finished. It is too important to ignore. So the person does what many competent people do when faced with an unfinishable inventory: they avoid looking at it, or they cherry-pick the easiest items, or they rewrite it to regain the feeling of control. The list becomes an emotional object rather than a practical one.

A shortlist respects reality.

The central claim here is not motivational. It is mechanical. A realistic task shortlist is a commitment device that aligns intended actions with actual time and energy. When the list matches capacity, the mind trusts it. Trust changes behaviour: fewer anxious checks, fewer guilt-driven rewrites, more steady follow-through. When the list exceeds capacity, the mind does not trust it and responds with monitoring, avoidance, or performative busyness. This is why a shortlist is not a sign of lowered ambition. It is a sign of accurate planning. Accurate planning reduces the attention leakage that has been accumulating since Chapter 1.

A scene from ordinary work makes the point sharper than theory. Someone begins the week with a long list and a vague sense that "this is what I need to do". They start Monday by responding to messages, because messages are visible and socially enforced. They glance at the list and feel the familiar pressure. Midday arrives and a few items have been ticked off, mostly small ones. The bigger items remain. They begin to feel heavier. By Tuesday evening, the list is still long, and the person begins to treat the list as an accusation. They stop consulting it because it makes them feel behind. The very tool meant to guide action has become something to hide from. The implication is practical: a list that induces avoidance has failed as a system, no matter how comprehensive it is.

The reason this happens lies partly in cognitive load. Every item on a list is not merely an action. It is a call on attention. Even when you are not doing the task, the task can impose a cost by existing as a reminder of obligation. Research on task switching has shown that shifting between tasks imposes costs in time and accuracy, even in relatively simple contexts (Rubinstein, Meyer, and Evans, 2001). An overlong list increases switching in a subtler way: it increases mental switching. The mind scans, compares, judges, postpones, reconsiders. It spends attention on selection rather than execution. This is why long lists can feel tiring even when little has been done. The list is demanding cognitive labour simply by being consulted.

A shortlist reduces this selection burden. It narrows the choice set so that the question "what should I do next?" becomes answerable without a miniature internal debate each time. It also reduces a specific form of risk: the risk of substituting easy tasks for meaningful ones. When the shortlist is constructed deliberately, it can include tasks that serve the week's chosen outcomes rather than merely clearing the inbox. This is not about being noble. It is about being coherent. A shortlist is a bridge between outcomes and daily action. Without it, outcomes remain aspirational headings while the week is swallowed by reactive tasks.

Energy is the other half of realism, and it is often ignored because it resists neat scheduling. Time is visible. Energy is less so, until it collapses. Many planning systems treat the day as a series of equal hours, as if attention and will were constant. They are not. Energy is uneven across the week, and it changes with sleep, stress, care demands, physical health, and emotional strain. This is not a medical claim. It is an observation of lived experience. A realistic shortlist accounts for this unevenness by avoiding the fantasy of doing deep work in your lowest-energy windows, or stacking emotionally demanding tasks back-to-back as if you were a machine. The implication is that a shortlist is not only about fewer items. It is about better matching between the kind of work and the likely quality of attention available.

The motif that holds this subchapter together is the suitcase. Packing a suitcase reveals how people really think about capacity. When faced with a limited space, most people do not attempt to bring everything they own. They choose. They pack what is essential, what is likely to be used, what fits the weather and the purpose of the trip. A week is a suitcase. You can cram it until the zip threatens to burst, but the bursting is not a moral lesson. It is physics. A realistic shortlist is the packing list that respects the suitcase. It prevents the week from starting with a zip already strained, which is how minor disruptions turn into collapses.

This is why long lists create guilt even in people who are doing a great deal. The guilt is not always about laziness. It is about implicit promises. A list reads, to the brain, like a set of commitments, even when the person insists it is "just a list". When those commitments are not met, the brain generates a social emotion towards the self: reproach. That reproach drains motivation and increases avoidance. A shortlist changes the emotional contract. It turns the list from "everything I could do" into "what I have decided I will attempt". The metric is behavioural. People with a shortlist tend to consult it more often because it does not punish them for looking. Consultation is a prerequisite for follow-through.

A second checkable example from outside personal organisation shows how capacity planning is treated as a serious discipline when the stakes are high. In manufacturing and operations, overloading a system beyond its capacity produces queues, delays, and quality problems. Taylor's era introduced many problematic assumptions about humans, but the basic idea that systems fail when overloaded is uncontroversial. Personal life is not a factory, yet the same dynamic holds. When a week is overloaded, tasks queue up, attention splinters, and quality suffers. A realistic shortlist is a form of capacity planning for a human system. It is not about squeezing more out of yourself. It is about reducing the overload that produces constant firefighting.

There is, however, a limitation worth naming because it prevents the shortlist from becoming dogma. Some roles and seasons generate genuine unpredictability: crisis work, caregiving volatility, heavy teaching loads, operational jobs with frequent interruptions. In such weeks, any shortlist can be disrupted. Insisting on a rigid plan can create stress that is disproportionate to its benefit. The reconciliation is to treat the shortlist as a flexible commitment rather than a brittle contract. Its purpose is not to eliminate disruption but to provide a baseline direction, a way to return to what matters after the inevitable interruptions. Even in volatile weeks, a shortlist can reduce decision fatigue by clarifying what deserves attention when a pocket of time appears.

Another limitation is that a shortlist can be used as a hiding place. People can make the shortlist so small and safe that it becomes an excuse to avoid meaningful work. This tends to happen when tasks are emotionally demanding or when the person fears failing. The suitcase becomes a toy suitcase. The reconciliation is to connect the shortlist to outcomes, not to comfort. If the shortlist is realistic but does not serve the week's intended results, it is merely a soothing ritual. The behavioural check is straightforward. At the end of the week, did the shortlist move anything that mattered, or did it simply create the feeling of being organised?

The suitcase motif returns when the week becomes crowded. The temptation is to add "just one more thing" repeatedly until the list becomes unfinishable. Each addition feels harmless in isolation. Cumulatively, it is how overload happens. A realistic shortlist requires the courage to say, not dramatically but firmly, "Not this week." That sentence is not procrastination. It is a declaration of capacity. It is also a protection for quality, because when too much is attempted, important tasks receive only fragments of attention, and fragments tend to produce rework.

The forward test is therefore not whether you can write down everything you want to do. It is whether you can pack the week without breaking the zip. When you look at your current list, which items are you carrying as a record of guilt rather than as a plan for action, and what would happen if you committed to a shortlist you could actually complete?

Parking longer projects

In September 1962 at Rice University in Houston, John F. Kennedy framed the United States space effort around a single, demanding outcome and did something else, less quoted but equally instructive: he implicitly admitted that certain ambitions require dedicated time, resources, and sequencing. A Moon programme could not be squeezed into the margins between other national tasks. It demanded blocks of attention, explicit commitments, and a willingness to treat long work as long work. When a society pretends that a major undertaking will happen in spare moments, the undertaking becomes myth. When a person pretends the same, the undertaking becomes guilt.

Big work needs a parking place.

The most corrosive lie in personal planning is the lie of the small gap. It sounds harmless. It even sounds optimistic. "I will do it when I have a moment." "I will catch up later." "I will chip away at it." Sometimes this is true for tasks that are genuinely small, runnable, and well-defined. For longer projects, it is often fantasy in polite clothing. Longer projects carry set-up costs, require sustained context, and generate follow-ups that cannot be resolved in scattered bursts. When they are repeatedly shoved into small gaps, they do not progress steadily. They fray. They create repeated restarts. They soak attention through constant low-level monitoring. They become the sort of open loop that follows you into the shower.

A scene from a typical week makes this painfully legible. Someone has a large task labelled in their system as if it were an action: "revise paper", "sort finances", "declutter home", "plan conference", "update portfolio", "fix website". It sits among smaller tasks like "reply to email" and "book appointment" as if it were a peer. The person feels virtuous for having written it down. Then they look for a free half-hour and try to begin. They spend ten minutes finding where they left off. They spend another ten remembering the state of play. They make a small adjustment, then an interruption arrives. The half-hour is gone. The project remains. Worse, it now carries residue: tabs opened, documents scattered, a faint sense of failure. The next attempt begins with the same set-up costs again. The concept here is context rebuilding. The implication is sharp: longer projects, placed into small gaps, charge you a toll each time you approach them, and the toll can consume the very time you hoped to use for progress.

Parking is the alternative to this toll. Parking is not procrastination. Parking is the deliberate act of assigning a longer project to an appropriate container: a separate plan, a dedicated block later, a project list that is reviewed weekly rather than daily, a scheduled session that acknowledges the project's true appetite for attention. Parking is a decision that turns vagueness into a stable state. It answers the brain's question: what happens next? The week becomes calmer when that question has a clear answer, because the mind stops pinging you with reminders that are really just distrust. The mind pings when it suspects a project will be forgotten. A parked project is less likely to be forgotten because it has a home.

The psychology behind this is not mysterious. When people face work that feels large and undefined, they experience what researchers have called decisional conflict and avoidance. The task is not only demanding; it is ambiguous. Ambiguity increases mental load because it forces continual micro-decisions about where to start, what matters, and what counts as progress. If the work is also important, the emotional stakes rise. High stakes plus ambiguity is a recipe for procrastination that looks like busyness: people do smaller tasks to regain a sense of competence. Parking interrupts this pattern by reframing the project as something that cannot be handled in the current context, and therefore should not be treated as a failing if it is not handled now. It is accurate planning.

A named, checkable example from outside personal life shows why parking is treated as standard practice in systems that cannot afford constant restarts. In software development, large changes are often organised into milestones, sprints, or separate branches precisely because they require sustained attention and coordination. Teams do not expect a major refactor to be done in "free moments" between bug fixes. They create a plan and reserve capacity. If they do not, the work stalls, conflicts accumulate, and the codebase becomes brittle. The personal analogue is immediate. A major household project, a research proposal, a long piece of writing, or a complicated administrative overhaul will not progress reliably if it is repeatedly pushed into the cracks of the day. You can attempt it. The system will punish you with rework.

The key idea is to stop pretending that all items on a task list are commensurate. They are not. Some items are actions. Some are projects. Treating projects as actions creates a persistent mismatch between expectation and reality. That mismatch breeds guilt. Guilt is not a motivational strategy. It tends to increase avoidance and reduce clarity. A more honest system distinguishes between the daily runnable tasks that fit into short periods and the longer projects that require a different mode of time. A project deserves a plan because it contains multiple decisions and dependencies. Without a plan, the mind must recreate the decisions each time, and recreation is waste.

This is also where the earlier discussion of "tiny tasks" becomes relevant again. Larger projects are not just longer. They often contain hidden micro-tasks that feel "tiny" but are actually blockers: find the right document, request the missing piece of information, decide on the structure, get agreement from someone else, locate the password, confirm the criteria. These blockers are the true next actions, and until they are named, the project feels like a fog. Parking a project does not mean ignoring these blockers. It means identifying the kind of work required and placing it where it can be done cleanly. Sometimes the right next action for a big project is genuinely small and can be done within the reset hour. Sometimes the right next action is to reserve a proper block later. Parking is the act of telling the truth about which is which.

The motif for this subchapter is the parking bay. A parking bay is not where you go to avoid driving. It is where you put a vehicle when you are not using it so it is not left blocking the road. A vehicle left half in the lane creates constant friction: other cars must weave around it, attention must be paid to it, annoyance rises. Many people leave their longer projects half in the lane. They keep them open in their minds and in their task lists, repeatedly bumping into them during the week. Parking moves the project out of the lane. It does not make the destination closer. It makes the road usable.

Parking also clarifies a subtle but crucial social reality: longer projects often involve other people. They require input, feedback, approval, coordination, shared calendars. When a project is treated as something that will happen "sometime", these social dependencies become sources of stress and delay. A person keeps thinking, "I must follow up," but does not, because they feel they have not made enough progress to justify the follow-up, or because they are uncertain what to ask for. When the project is parked properly, its dependencies become explicit. They can be placed on a waiting-for list. They can be followed up in a contained way. The project becomes less emotionally charged because it is no longer a shapeless cloud hanging over the week.

A limitation must be faced, otherwise parking sounds like an excuse. Some people park projects permanently. They create a graveyard of worthy intentions: books to write, finances to sort, relationships to repair, homes to reorganise, papers to draft. Parking becomes avoidance when it is not paired with any credible next engagement. The reconciliation is to treat parking as a state that must include a retrieval mechanism, however modest: a scheduled block, a reviewed project list, a dedicated note that will be consulted during the weekly reset. The aim is not to force immediate progress. The aim is to prevent the project from hovering in the lane, draining attention while never moving.

Another limitation is that life does sometimes allow meaningful progress in small gaps, particularly for certain kinds of work that can be modularised cleanly. Some researchers write notes in transit. Some writers draft paragraphs in short sessions. Some domestic projects can be advanced through quick, well-defined micro-actions. The distinction is not the length of the gap but the cost of re-entry. If re-entry costs are low, small gaps can be useful. If re-entry costs are high, small gaps are expensive. Parking is therefore not an absolute rule. It is a diagnosis of re-entry friction. The metric is again behavioural: if each attempt begins with long reorientation and ends with minimal progress, the project is not suited to gaps. It needs a bay and a longer run.

There is also a moral shift here that matters for sustainability. When people stop pretending a project will fit into the cracks, they stop lying to themselves, and that honesty reduces shame. Shame is a powerful blocker because it makes the project feel like evidence of inadequacy. A parked project, handled accurately, becomes simply a piece of work awaiting the right conditions. This reframing protects self-respect and reduces the mental pinging that comes from distrust. The mind relaxes when it believes you are being truthful about capacity.

The parking bay motif returns in the moment of Sunday planning when the temptation is strongest. The list of tasks is in front of you. A large project sits there like an uninvited guest. You can either pretend it will be handled "somehow" and carry it half in the road all week, or you can park it properly and accept the discomfort of not pretending. The forward test is sharp: which project have you been dragging along the lane for weeks, and what would change if you gave it a real bay and a real plan for retrieval rather than another week of hopeful hovering?

Chapter 6
Calendar planning that holds up

A person plans Monday with a kind of brittle optimism. The calendar looks orderly. There are neat blocks. Each block is pressed up against the next like books on a shelf. The day has no gaps, which feels efficient, almost elegant. Then reality arrives. A meeting runs long. A train is delayed. A child needs collecting. A call that should have been quick becomes complicated. The first slip forces a small scramble, the second slip forces a larger one, and by lunchtime the schedule has collapsed into improvisation. The person is not surprised by the existence of disruption. They are surprised by how quickly one disruption ruins everything.

Another person plans the same day with looser edges and still feels frustrated. They leave gaps, but the gaps are swallowed by low-value tasks, the kind that breed when time looks available: checking messages, tidying, admin, the useful-but-not-urgent work that expands because it can. When the moment arrives for deep focus, there is none left. The calendar looks kinder than the first person's, yet it still fails to protect what matters. The day ends with a familiar ache: busy, exhausted, and oddly dissatisfied.

Time is not the only variable.

That is the central tension. Most calendar planning fails either because it ignores constraints or because it ignores energy. Ignoring constraints produces fragility: the plan cannot absorb normal delay. Ignoring energy produces cruelty: the plan asks for deep concentration at times when attention is predictably thin. In both cases, the person experiences the failure as personal: "I cannot stick to my plan." Yet the plan itself may be the culprit. A calendar that holds up is not a fantasy of control. It is a design that respects what cannot move and what cannot be forced.

The stakes are immediate because the calendar is where commitments become real. Lists are intentions. Calendars are promises. When the calendar is inaccurate, people lose not only time but trust: trust in their own planning, trust in their availability, trust in their ability to show up. That loss of trust has predictable behavioural consequences. People start double-checking, constantly. They hesitate before agreeing to anything because they fear hidden collisions. They overbook and then apologise. They underbook and then drift. A robust calendar reduces the need for this monitoring because it behaves like a reliable map rather than a decorative timetable.

The deeper stakes are about what a week feels like from the inside. A fragile calendar produces a particular kind of stress: anticipatory stress. The person looks at the day and senses that any delay will cause failure, so they begin already tense, already rushing. That tension changes behaviour: impatience increases, errors rise, communication becomes sharper, relationships take strain. A cruel calendar produces a different stress: moral stress. The person repeatedly asks themselves to do demanding work in low-energy windows, then judges themselves when they cannot. Both stresses are avoidable, not through greater grit, but through better design. Design here means acknowledging that time has friction and attention has rhythm.

This chapter continues the book's broader argument about control without perfection. Control is not achieved by filling every minute. Control is achieved by creating a plan that can survive contact with life. Survival requires buffers, not as indulgence, but as shock absorbers. It also requires a more honest understanding of capacity, not as a fixed number of hours but as variable quality of attention. A calendar that holds up is one that anticipates ordinary disruption and protects the most important work by placing it where you can actually do it. The plan becomes less impressive and more true.

The motif for this chapter is the hinge. A calendar without buffers is a hinge without play: it binds and then snaps under pressure. A calendar without energy-awareness is a hinge installed the wrong way round: it technically moves, but not smoothly, and you end up forcing it. The hinge matters because the week is not a continuous sheet of time. It is a series of transitions: from home to work, from meeting to focus, from care responsibilities to admin, from day to evening. Transitions have costs. Ignoring those costs creates plans that look possible on paper and fail in practice. A well-designed hinge acknowledges movement and makes it easier.

The path in this chapter begins by placing hard commitments where they belong: the appointments, deadlines, travel, and care responsibilities that anchor the week and cannot be negotiated away. It then turns to the less visible constraint that determines whether the plan will be lived or merely admired: the distribution of focus and energy, and how tasks can be placed so demanding work is not scheduled into predictable low-attention windows. Together, these moves change the calendar from a wish list into a workable contract with reality.

The unresolved friction that pulls us into the practical work is both simple and revealing. When your calendar collapses, does it usually collapse because one delay knocks everything out of place, or because the plan asks you to do your hardest thinking at the very times you most reliably run out of it?

Hard commitments first

On 15 January 2009, US Airways Flight 1549 struck birds after take-off from LaGuardia Airport in New York City and lost thrust in both engines. Chesley Sullenberger and Jeffrey Skiles had minutes to respond, and their options were not defined by aspiration but by constraints: altitude, airspeed, distance, water, gravity. The outcome is well known, yet the instructive point for ordinary planning is quieter. Under pressure, competent people do not begin with what they would *like* to do. They begin with what cannot be wished away. They map the immovable facts first.

Constraints come first.

A calendar that holds up is built on the same principle, only with far less drama. Hard commitments are the immovable facts of a week: appointments you must attend, deadlines with external consequences, travel time that exists whether you respect it or not, care responsibilities that do not pause because your inbox is busy. When people plan without placing these commitments first, they build on air. They fill the week with "work blocks" and optimistic tasks, then discover the hard commitments later, when the clash forces a scramble. The scramble is not evidence of a chaotic life. It is evidence of a plan that ignored constraints.

A scene from ordinary life shows how quickly ignoring constraints creates stress. Someone books meetings back-to-back, then adds a personal appointment in the middle of the day, assuming it will "fit". They forget the travel time. They forget the time needed to leave one conversation, gather themselves, and arrive. They forget the uncertainty: trains run late, lifts are slow, traffic is moody, people stop you in corridors. The day becomes brittle. A single delay turns into a cascade, and the person spends the rest of the afternoon apologising, rushing, and losing attention. The concept here is schedule fragility. The implication is blunt. A schedule that cannot absorb normal friction will manufacture emergencies.

Hard commitments deserve to be mapped first for two reasons. The first is collision prevention. Collisions are not merely inconvenient; they are reputational and relational hazards. They create missed calls, rescheduled appointments, late arrivals, and that sour feeling of being unreliable even when you care deeply about showing up. The second reason is resource realism. Hard commitments do not merely occupy time; they consume energy and attention. A demanding meeting can drain the cognitive reserve needed for deep work. A travel-heavy day is not equivalent to a desk day, even if the calendar shows the same number of hours "free". Planning that begins with hard commitments therefore produces a more accurate sense of what the week can truly hold.

The language of "hard" can mislead, as if these commitments are always formal. Many are informal and therefore easy to omit. The school pick-up that must happen at a certain time. The relative who needs a weekly check-in. The recurring care duty that cannot be shifted without consequences. The household tasks that keep a home functional. These are hard commitments too. They are time-bound and socially meaningful. When they are left out of the calendar, the calendar becomes a fantasy document, and the person is forced to manage reality through last-minute improvisation. The implication is that the calendar is only as trustworthy as the commitments it contains, including the ones that do not come with an official invitation.

Buffers exist to protect hard commitments from the ordinary friction of life. Without buffers, a hard commitment becomes a brittle spike in the day: everything must be perfect for it to be met without stress. With buffers, the commitment becomes robust: it can be met even when something runs long. The phrase "a ten-minute buffer can save an hour of stress" is not a numerical claim about guaranteed outcomes; it is a statement about cascade prevention. Cascades are what make days feel ruined. A small buffer can interrupt a cascade by giving the schedule room to breathe, room to absorb a delay without forcing immediate triage. The behavioural metric is clear. Fewer frantic messages. Fewer rushed transitions. Fewer apologies. More arrivals that feel calm rather than breathless.

The logic of buffers is well understood in domains where scheduling errors have visible costs. Transport systems build slack into timetables because small delays propagate.

Manufacturing systems maintain safety stock because supply disruptions cascade. In project management, critical path thinking identifies tasks that constrain the entire timeline and treats them differently because their delay has disproportionate consequences. You do not need a formal methodology to benefit from the principle. The principle is simply this: some commitments constrain the day, and the safest way to handle constraints is to protect them against variability. Variability is not a moral flaw. It is the world.

A second checkable example shows how institutional systems treat buffers as a form of responsibility rather than indulgence. In aviation, turnaround times and flight schedules include built-in slack because weather, air traffic control, and maintenance variability are unavoidable. Airlines and airports may argue about how much slack is economical, but the idea that schedules must include contingency is not controversial. A pilot does not plan a flight assuming perfect conditions. They plan with alternates. They carry reserves. The implication for a personal calendar is not to mimic an airline. It is to respect that your week, too, has weather: interruptions, delays, unpredictable human needs. A buffer is an alternate route for your day.

Putting hard commitments first also clarifies what the "free time" actually is. People often look at an empty patch of calendar and assume it is available for demanding work. Yet the empty patch might be bordered by two hard commitments that require mental transitions: leaving one context, preparing for another, travelling, recovering. A schedule that ignores transitions produces the illusion of free time and then punishes the person for failing to use it as imagined. When hard commitments are placed first and protected, the remaining time becomes more honest. It might be less. It will be truer. Truth is what reduces background stress, because truth reduces the need for constant recalculation.

There is a limitation worth admitting, because hard commitments can be used as an excuse to avoid important work. Some people fill their calendars with meetings and errands until there is no space left for the tasks that actually require thinking. Hard commitments can be real and still be mismanaged. The reconciliation is to treat "hard commitments first" as sequencing, not as surrender. Placing hard commitments first is a way of seeing the week clearly, not a way of declaring that nothing else matters. It is the groundwork that allows deliberate choices about what fits around those commitments, rather than letting the week be shaped entirely by whoever books time first or whoever demands attention most loudly.

Another limitation is practical. Some hard commitments are unpredictable, especially in caregiving and operational roles. The exact timing of demands can shift. In such lives, the calendar cannot become a rigid script. Yet the principle still holds. Even if exact times vary, the existence of constraints does not. A person may not know precisely when the disruption will land, but they may know which days are likely to be volatile and which windows tend to be eaten by care. Mapping those realities is still useful because it prevents planning deep work into predictable chaos and then treating the resulting failure as personal weakness. Constraints are not excuses. They are data.

The quiet motif for this subchapter is the anchor. Hard commitments are anchors in the week. An anchor holds. If you pretend an anchor is not there, you will still feel its pull, only later, as a sudden jerk when the chain goes taut. Place the anchors first, and you can plot the rest of the course with less drama. Ignore them, and the day becomes a series of last-minute adjustments to forces you always knew existed.

The forward test is direct. When you look at your calendar for the week ahead, are the anchors visible and protected, or are they hidden, leaving you to discover their weight only when the chain pulls tight at the worst moment?

Matching tasks to energy

On 24 March 1989 in Prince William Sound, Alaska, the oil tanker *Exxon Valdez* ran aground on Bligh Reef and spilled crude oil into the water. In the aftermath, investigations and reporting repeatedly returned to a theme that is as ordinary as it is uncomfortable: human performance varies, and fatigue and watchstanding conditions can shape what people notice, decide, and miss. The sea air can smell clean and sharp; diesel is not. Catastrophe is rarely caused by a single bad person doing a single bad thing. It is often the product of a system that asks for high judgement when human capacity is low.

Energy is not optional.

Most weeks do not involve reefs and tankers, yet many personal calendars are built on the same faulty assumption: that attention is available on demand. People plan as if "free time" were a neutral container, equally suitable for drafting a complex paper, negotiating a sensitive conversation, or doing routine admin. Then the plan collapses in a familiar way. The demanding task is postponed again and again because the hour in which it was scheduled turns out to be an hour when the brain is foggy, the body is tired, or the day has already spent its best attention on meetings, commuting, and other people's priorities. The person concludes they are undisciplined. The calendar, quietly, has been lying.

A schedule that ignores energy invites self-contempt because it sets up repeated failure. The failure is predictable. A human being does not carry the same cognitive power through every part of a day. Focus has rhythms. There are peaks when complex reasoning feels possible and troughs when even a simple email feels oddly heavy. When a plan treats those troughs as ideal moments for deep work, it turns ordinary biology into a moral problem. That is how people end up living in a cycle of overpromising, underdelivering, and then trying to compensate with longer hours, frantic last-minute work, and the constant hum of "I should be doing more".

The alternative begins with a less flattering, more accurate definition of "capacity". Capacity is not simply how many hours appear empty on a calendar. It is how much usable attention exists inside those hours. This is why energy-aware planning is kinder and more workable. Kindness here is not softness. It is precision. It respects that certain tasks demand concentrated attention, emotional regulation, or creative synthesis, and that these forms of effort cannot be summoned reliably in every window. When tasks are matched to energy, the person is not forced to wrestle themselves into performance. They are placed in conditions where performance is more likely.

A simple scene shows the difference in behaviour. One person schedules their hardest thinking late in the day because that is when the calendar looks open. The slot arrives after a dense sequence of meetings and decisions. They sit down, open the document, and immediately drift. They re-read paragraphs without absorbing them. They check messages "for a minute". They start reformatting rather than writing, because formatting is controllable. They emerge later with little progress and a feeling of dull defeat. Another person schedules demanding work in a window when they tend to feel mentally sharper, even if that window is shorter or requires firmer protection. When the slot arrives, the document is approached with less resistance. The person still has to work, but they are not fighting the same internal drag. The implication is not that energy-aware planning guarantees success. It is that it reduces friction, and reduced friction is often the difference between consistent progress and perpetual postponement.

The scientific underpinning for this is not mysterious, even if the lived experience often feels personal. In 2017 in Stockholm, the Nobel Prize in Physiology or Medicine was awarded to Jeffrey C. Hall, Michael Rosbash, and Michael W. Young for discoveries of molecular mechanisms controlling circadian rhythm (Nobel Prize, 2017). Circadian rhythm is the body's internal timing system, affecting sleep-wake cycles and broader patterns of alertness. The point here is not to turn the Sunday reset into a chronobiology seminar. It is to legitimise what people already know in their bones: attention has a timetable, even when the diary pretends it does not. When you plan without regard to that timetable, you create a week that requires constant self-overriding. Self-overriding is exhausting.

The crucial move is to treat energy as a constraint in the same way Chapter 6 treated hard commitments as constraints. A deadline is a constraint. A school pick-up is a constraint. Your own predictable low-energy windows are constraints too. They are not excuses. They are conditions. When conditions are ignored, plans become brittle. When conditions are respected, plans become robust. Robustness shows up in visible metrics of behaviour: fewer abandoned work sessions, fewer late-night rescue efforts, fewer times you "start" the same task without moving it forward, fewer anxious checks prompted by the fear that the day is slipping away.

Energy-aware planning also sharpens the urgent/important distinction from the previous chapter. When people are tired, they gravitate towards the urgent-looking and easy-to-finish, because tired minds crave quick relief. This is not laziness; it is an adaptive response. The problem appears when the calendar repeatedly places important demanding work into tired windows, ensuring that the tired mind will repeatedly choose relief instead. The week then becomes a chain of substitutions: emails instead of analysis, tidying instead of drafting, small admin instead of the project that matters. Matching tasks to energy interrupts this by placing the important work where it has a fighting chance, and placing the lower-cognitive-load work where it can be completed without damaging self-trust.

A second named example, closer to everyday knowledge work, makes the social side of this clearer. In 2001, researchers Rubinstein, Meyer, and Evans published work on task switching that highlighted performance costs when people move between tasks (Rubinstein, Meyer, and Evans, 2001). Even without quoting figures, the implication is intuitive: switching exacts a toll. Energy dips make switching more likely because sustained focus is harder to hold. If your calendar stacks high-switching, interruption-prone activities into your most fragile windows, the day will feel like it is constantly slipping. If it places sustained work into a window with fewer interruptions and higher alertness, the cognitive toll is lower. The result is not merely better output. It is less mental residue.

This is where "efficiency" deserves a more human definition. Efficiency is often imagined as speed, as squeezing more tasks into less time. Energy-aware planning treats efficiency as reduced waste: fewer false starts, fewer sessions where you sit down to work and end up reorienting yourself for most of the time, fewer times you postpone something important because you have scheduled it in a window where it will predictably fail. Waste is visible. It looks like reopened documents, repeated re-reading, lists rewritten because the week has drifted, and that weary sensation of having been busy without having progressed. When you match tasks to energy, you reduce these waste patterns not by trying harder, but by asking the right kind of work to happen at the right kind of time.

The quiet motif worth keeping is the battery. A battery is not moral. It has charge or it does not. You can run a device until the battery is low, but the device will then perform poorly, and blaming the device changes nothing. Many people treat their attention like a battery they can shame into charging. They schedule intellectually demanding work in depleted windows and then feel astonished by their own resistance. Energy-aware planning is simply the refusal to confuse a depleted battery with a defective character. It does not mean never doing hard things when tired; life will require that sometimes. It means not building a week that requires it constantly.

There is, of course, a limitation. Not everyone has stable daily rhythms, and not everyone's energy is predictable week to week. Shift work, caregiving volatility, travel, chronic stress, and fluctuating life demands can make "best hours" feel like a luxury concept. In such contexts, energy-aware planning cannot rely on neat regularity. The reconciliation is to broaden the idea: even if energy is variable, some contexts are still more supportive than others. Certain windows are consistently interruption-heavy. Certain times are consistently fragmented. Certain parts of the day reliably involve transitions that drain attention. Matching tasks to energy, here, becomes matching tasks to *conditions*: choosing to place demanding work away from predictably chaotic zones, even if you cannot guarantee a perfect "high energy" slot.

Another limitation is that some urgent demands ignore energy completely. A hard deadline can arrive when you are depleted. A family need can override any plan. Energy-aware planning does not pretend you can opt out of reality. It changes what happens around those moments. If the calendar has acknowledged your hard commitments and your likely low-energy windows, then when disruption occurs you have less re-planning to do. You know what can move and what cannot. You know which tasks require charge and which tasks are more tolerant of depletion. That clarity reduces panic, which itself is an energy drain.

Energy matching also has a relational dimension that is easy to miss. When you consistently schedule demanding work at the wrong time, you become more irritable and less present in the rest of your life. The cost is not confined to productivity. It shows up as sharper replies, shorter patience, and the subtle feeling that everyone is competing with your depleted attention. A kinder calendar protects not only your work but your relationships, because it reduces the number of times you are forced to do difficult things while running on fumes. This is not sentimental. It is preventive.

The battery motif returns in the most practical way. A well-planned week does not aim to keep the battery at full charge. That is fantasy. It aims to avoid repeatedly attempting high-drain tasks when the battery is already low, because that pattern produces failure, shame, and more depletion. Instead, it places high-drain work where there is charge and low-drain work where there is less. The week becomes less heroic and more reliable.

The forward test is therefore not whether you can push through tiredness when necessary. Most people can, and do. The question is whether your calendar is quietly built on the expectation that you will push through tiredness all week, or whether it respects the battery enough to place your most demanding work where your best attention is most likely to exist.

Chapter 7
A task system you trust

A person opens their task list and feels an unexpected surge of irritation. Not at the work itself, but at the list. The items stare back in a strange, accusatory shorthand: "sort finances", "deal with email", "health stuff", "house admin", "project", "follow up". The list is long, yet oddly unhelpful. It does not tell them what to do next. It tells them what they have been avoiding. They scroll, hoping for an obvious starting point, and the scroll becomes a kind of self-soothing. The day passes. The list remains.

Another person has a different problem. Their list is beautifully organised. It has categories and labels and clever naming conventions. It feels like a system. Yet the system demands maintenance. New tasks arrive and must be filed. Old tasks must be reviewed and rewritten. The list becomes a garden that needs constant weeding, and the gardener starts to prefer gardening to harvesting. The person experiences this as being organised, yet the same core question returns at inconvenient moments: what, precisely, should I do now?

The system is either trusted or it is not.

That is the central tension. A task system is not a repository of intentions. It is an instrument for action. If it does not reliably produce the next doable step, it becomes a source of mental noise rather than relief. People then compensate in predictable ways. They keep tasks in their heads "just in case". They leave messages unread as crude reminders. They duplicate tasks across tools. They rewrite their list to regain the feeling of control. Each compensation increases attention leakage, which is the opposite of what this book has been trying to reduce. The aim is not to have a perfect list. The aim is to have a list the mind believes.

Trust matters because it changes behaviour without requiring heroism. When the system is trusted, you consult it calmly. You act. You stop thinking about what you have stored because you know you can retrieve it. When the system is not trusted, you monitor. You check. You worry. You keep running internal backups. The person may look organised, yet their attention remains on call. A trusted system is quiet. It does its job in the background. It creates a small, steady confidence that the week is not being managed by memory and panic.

A task system becomes untrustworthy for three predictable reasons. The first is vagueness. Vague tasks are not tasks; they are labels for unease. They do not tell you what to do. They tell you that a domain of life is unsettled. Vague tasks trigger avoidance because they require multiple decisions before any action can begin. The second is overcomplexity. Too many categories, tags, and folders create friction at the point of capture and retrieval. The system becomes another job. The third is cosmetic maintenance. People rewrite their lists instead of making decisions, because rewriting feels productive while allowing the work to remain safely abstract. The list becomes more beautiful and less useful.

The stakes are not trivial. A vague or overcomplex system tends to produce two kinds of failure that quietly corrode self-trust. The first is drift: the person keeps doing what is most immediate and socially enforced, while important but non-urgent work languishes because the list does not surface it clearly. The second is guilt: the person carries a long inventory of "shoulds" that never become concrete actions, and the mind begins to associate the list with failure. Guilt increases avoidance, avoidance increases backlog, backlog increases monitoring. The loop tightens. A trusted system breaks this loop by making action easier than avoidance.

The motif for this chapter is the handle. A task without a handle cannot be picked up. People keep staring at it, circling it, thinking about it, but they cannot lift it cleanly because it lacks a clear point of contact. A clear next action is a handle. A simple category structure is a set of hooks you can reach for without thinking. A review practice that does not devolve into rewriting is a way of keeping the handles visible rather than sanding them down into vague polish. A handle does not make the work pleasant. It makes the work possible.

This chapter continues the book's insistence on control without perfection. A trusted task system is not an ornate framework. It is a practical object that serves the week. It reduces searching, reduces rethinking, reduces the urge to keep everything in mind. It also respects the constraint that the Sunday reset is one hour. Any task system that requires lengthy maintenance will not survive. The question is not whether a system can be made sophisticated. The question is whether it can remain usable when you are tired, distracted, and carrying other responsibilities.

The path here moves from blur to specificity, from the vague intention that triggers avoidance to the single-sitting action that can actually be done. It then moves into structure, not the intoxicating complexity of endless labels, but a small set of categories that make tasks findable without turning organisation into a hobby. It ends with a way of refreshing the system that protects it from becoming a shrine to order, keeping the emphasis on decisions and scheduling rather than on endless rearrangement.

The unresolved friction that pulls us into the practical work is simple enough to be diagnostic. When you look at your list, do you feel a clean sense of "I know what to do next", or do you feel a dull pressure to rewrite the list until it looks like control?

Writing clear next actions

In 1911 in Philadelphia, Frederick Winslow Taylor published *The Principles of Scientific Management* and insisted that vague exhortations were a poor substitute for clear, observable work (Taylor, 1911). Taylor's conclusions about people were often too mechanistic, but one narrow point remains useful: when a task is described in a way that cannot be executed, it is not a task at all. It is a wish. Wishes sit on lists for months. Executable actions move.

Vagueness is sticky.

That stickiness is why "blur tasks" clog even the most sophisticated systems. A blur task looks like work, sounds like work, and carries the emotional weight of work, but it does not tell you what to do when you sit down. "Sort finances." "Deal with email." "Fix the website." "Plan the trip." "Improve fitness." "Research the options." Each phrase is a label for a domain of life. It is not a next move. When a person sees it on their list, the brain recognises the size and complexity hiding behind the words and quietly recoils. The recoil is not laziness. It is the nervous system refusing an ill-defined demand.

A clear next action is different. It is specific enough to begin without further decisions, small enough to be done in one sitting, and concrete enough that the mind can imagine the first step. "Find last month's statement." "Search inbox for the appointment email." "Draft the three questions to ask." "Open the folder and locate the latest version." "Send the message confirming Tuesday." The difference is not motivation. It is handle design. A blur task has no handle. A clear next action does. You can pick it up.

The cognitive logic is straightforward. When you face a blur task, you are not merely facing work. You are facing a stack of hidden decisions: what exactly counts as "sorted", what information is needed, which system to use, where to begin, what order to do things in, what to do if something goes wrong. Hidden decisions create friction. Friction creates avoidance. Avoidance creates the familiar cycle of guilt and repeated mental pings. By contrast, a clear next action collapses the decision stack into a single move. It reduces the need for the brain to negotiate with itself. The implication is practical and immediate: clarity does not just make tasks easier to do; it makes them easier to *start*, and starting is often the true barrier.

A scene from a normal Monday reveals the mechanism. A person has a spare hour between two meetings. They open their task list. Near the top is "sort finances". They feel a slight sinking sensation. The phrase implies bank logins, documents, uncertain spending, possible mistakes, and the possibility of discovering something unpleasant. Their brain offers a substitute: answer emails. Emails are concrete. Each one has a visible prompt and a clear response. They reply to several, feel productive, and the hour evaporates. "Sort finances" remains untouched, now with a thicker layer of shame. The concept here is substitution under ambiguity. The implication is that blur tasks do not merely fail to be completed; they actively steer attention towards lower-value work because the mind prefers the relief of the doable to the discomfort of the undefined.

There is evidence that unfinished goals can generate intrusive thoughts and that making a plan can reduce those intrusions. Masicampo and Baumeister reported that unfulfilled goals increased intrusive thoughts and that forming a plan could reduce them (Masicampo and Baumeister, 2011). A clear next action is a tiny plan. It answers the question "what will happen next?" with enough specificity that the mind can stop monitoring the task as a threat. Monitoring is costly. It shows up as repeated rechecking, avoidance, and that low-level buzz of "I must not forget". When the next move is clear, the buzz reduces. The mind trusts that the task has a runway.

Clarity also changes the social dynamics of work. Many blur tasks are social in disguise. "Follow up on project" might actually mean "ask for the missing input" or "tell someone the decision". Vague phrasing lets people avoid the social discomfort of making a request or stating a boundary. The task stays on the list as a form of moral signalling: I care about this. Meanwhile, nothing changes in the world. A clear next action forces contact with reality. It turns vague intention into a message, a call, a decision, a scheduled meeting, a delegated request. The implication is that clarity can be emotionally harder than vagueness because it requires committing to a specific social act. That hardness is often why clarity is avoided, which is precisely why it is valuable.

Two named examples help anchor this beyond personal habit talk. The first is the origin of the checklist. After the 30 October 1935 crash of the Boeing Model 299 at Wright Field in Dayton, Ohio, aviation culture increasingly relied on checklists to prevent omission in complex tasks. The central insight was not that pilots were careless. It was that complexity exceeds memory, and that small, explicit steps reduce errors. A clear next action is a personal checklist item. It transforms "prepare" into "confirm fuel valve position", "set flaps", "remove gust lock". The implication for life admin is not to dramatise your errands as aviation. It is to treat clarity as a safety mechanism against omission and procrastination, because omission often begins with vagueness.

The second is organisational. GOV.UK, launched in October 2012 in the UK, was built around making user journeys clear: "Start now" rather than a thicket of vague options. The design choice was to reduce cognitive load by presenting the next step plainly. People do not fail to use government services because they are incapable; they fail because the path is unclear, and unclear paths invite abandonment. Personal tasks behave similarly. If the next step is not visible, the task will be deferred, and deferral becomes a form of hidden cost: re-reading, re-deciding, and re-remembering. The implication is that a good task system is less like a library catalogue and more like a signposted path.

The most common misunderstanding about clear next actions is that they must be tiny. They do not. They must be *runnable.*

A runnable action is one you can execute without further clarification. It might still take effort. It might still be unpleasant. It might still require concentration. But it is defined. This distinction matters because some people respond to the call for clarity by fragmenting everything into micro-steps until the list becomes absurd and demoralising. They create a bureaucracy of action. The list becomes unmanageable, and the person retreats into avoidance again. The aim is not atomisation. The aim is to remove the ambiguity that blocks starting.

The right granularity is therefore a judgement call. One sitting is the guiding constraint, not because every task should be short, but because one sitting forces a task to have a clear boundary. "Write the report" is not one sitting unless it is a very short report. "Draft the introduction paragraph" might be. "Open the report document and outline the sections" might be. "Email the supervisor with two clarifying questions" might be. The point is that the action must end somewhere, so completion is recognisable. Recognisability matters because it produces closure, and closure reduces mental noise. The mind calms when it can say, truthfully, "That is done."

A credible limitation must be admitted, because clarity has its own risks. Some work is inherently exploratory. Research, creative writing, complex problem-solving, and strategic thinking often begin in fog, and forcing an artificial clarity too early can produce premature closure, pushing the work into simplistic steps that miss the real problem. This is not an excuse for vagueness in life admin. It is a reminder that clarity must be used where it serves the work. The reconciliation is to distinguish between tasks whose purpose is execution and tasks whose purpose is exploration. Execution tasks need clear next actions because they are about moving something through the world. Exploration tasks may need a different kind of next action: "read for twenty minutes and take notes", "write a rough outline", "generate three options", "formulate the question". Even exploration benefits from a runnable action, but the action's output is information, not completion.

Clarity also interacts with perfectionism. People sometimes refuse to define a next action because defining it feels like committing to a plan that might be wrong. They keep the task vague as a way to avoid being pinned down. This is especially common among thoughtful professionals who fear wasting time on the wrong direction. Yet vagueness is not neutrality. It is a cost. It produces repeated rumination and delays any learning that would come from action. A clear next action is not a declaration that the whole project is known. It is simply the next experiment. The implication is that clarity can be humble. It can define the next move without pretending to define the entire journey.

The motif worth keeping is the handle. When you look at your list, you can feel which items have handles and which are slippery. Handle-less tasks create hesitation. Hesitation is where avoidance begins. A handle gives the mind something to grasp, which means the mind can stop circling and start moving. Movement reduces noise because it produces state changes. State changes are what your brain recognises as progress, and progress is what quietens the ping.

The forward test is therefore not whether you can write attractive tasks. It is whether you can write runnable ones. When you scan your list, which items are blur tasks that make you flinch, and what would they become if you forced them to grow a handle: a single, concrete next action you could do in one sitting?

Using simple categories

In London in October 2012, the UK Government Digital Service launched GOV.UK with a design philosophy that resisted the temptation to mirror the full complexity of government departments. The decision was structural: present information through a coherent set of user-facing categories and journeys rather than forcing citizens to understand internal bureaucratic boundaries. The point was not to make government simpler than it is. The point was to make it *findable*. Findability reduces friction. Friction creates drop-off. A task list behaves the same way, only the citizen is you.

Too many labels slow you.

People begin categorising tasks for a sensible reason. Without categories, a list becomes a landfill: items pile up and searching takes too long. With some categories, tasks become easier to retrieve in the moment they can be done. "Calls" can be tackled when you have a phone and privacy. "Errands" can be tackled when you are out. "Home" can be tackled when you are in the house with access to the right things. These categories do not make you disciplined. They make you less likely to forget and less likely to waste time deciding where to start. The surprise is that categorising can also become a trap. Too many labels produce a second job: maintaining the categories.

The central tension is between organisation that reduces effort and organisation that *creates* effort. A few categories act like signage. A proliferation of categories becomes a maze. The mind is then forced to do the very thing the system was meant to prevent: make decisions and switch contexts at the point of use. If every task must be tagged precisely, the capture process slows and becomes negotiable, which leads to inconsistent capture, which leads to mistrust, which leads to attention leakage. A system designed to relieve the mind becomes another open loop: "I should really organise my tasks better." That is not a task. It is a warning sign.

A scene makes this immediate. Someone has a task list with dozens of labels: work, personal, admin, deep work, shallow work, phone, email, computer, home, errands, urgent, later, waiting, reading, writing, thinking, planning, financial, health, family, household, and on it goes, each label created with good intentions. A new task arrives: "send the document." The person hesitates. Is it work or admin? Is it email or computer? Is it urgent or later? The hesitation seems small, but it repeats. Eventually, capture becomes a tax. The person starts dumping tasks without tagging, promising to sort them later. Later does not arrive. Now the system contains a mix of well-tagged and untagged items, which makes it unreliable. Reliability collapses not because the person lacks character, but because the system asks too much in the moments when life is busy.

The name for this problem is overhead. Overhead is the extra effort required to keep a system running that does not directly advance the work. Overhead is not always bad; some is necessary. The point is that overhead must be proportionate. In personal task management, overhead becomes dangerous when it competes with execution. You can measure this without numbers. If you spend more time categorising and recategorising than you spend doing, overhead has won. If your list becomes a place you "maintain" rather than a tool you use, overhead has won. The implication is that the best categories are not the cleverest. They are the ones that require the least thought to apply and still reduce searching later.

Simple categories work because they map to contexts that are stable in real life. Context here does not mean a philosophical setting; it means the practical conditions required to do a task: location, tools, time window, and social privacy. A phone call requires quiet and perhaps emotional readiness. An errand requires leaving the house. A household task requires being at home and having access to the relevant objects. Work tasks often require a different cognitive stance than domestic tasks, even when done at the same kitchen table. When categories map to these stable contexts, they reduce the chance of forgetting because they allow you to batch tasks in moments when the context is already available. The behaviour you observe is a reduction in "wasted starts": fewer times you attempt a task and then realise you cannot do it because you lack the right conditions.

This is also why categories should be few. The point of a category is to speed retrieval, not to describe a task's soul. When categories become descriptive rather than functional, they become decorative. "High impact" sounds useful but is often subjective in the moment. "Strategic" can be an ego label. "Deep work" is a noble tag that can become a hiding place if you never schedule it. The task system should serve the week, not inflate the self-image of the person using it. Simple categories resist self-deception by being blunt: phone, home, errands, work. Blunt categories are harder to argue with, and argument is a form of friction.

A second checkable example from information science helps explain why too many categories are not just annoying but cognitively expensive. In 1956, George A. Miller published "The Magical Number Seven, Plus or Minus Two", discussing limits in immediate memory capacity (Miller, 1956). The paper has been debated and refined in subsequent research, but the basic message remains useful at the level of lived experience: there are limits to how many distinct things the mind can hold and manipulate at once. A sprawling category system asks the mind to remember too much at the moment of use. It increases cognitive load precisely when you are trying to reduce it. The implication is not that you must have exactly a certain number of categories. The implication is that simpler systems respect cognitive limits, while ornate systems exploit them.

Categories also influence how you perceive your commitments. A list without categories can feel like an undifferentiated mass, which triggers avoidance. A list with too many categories can feel like a library catalogue, impressive but hard to use quickly. A list with a few categories feels like a set of drawers. You can open the drawer that fits your current context and choose from a smaller set. This reduces decision fatigue. Decision fatigue is not a mystical depletion of will; it is the ordinary effect of making too many choices and comparisons. When you reduce the number of choices, you reduce the fatigue. The result is not merely higher output. It is calmer attention.

There is, however, a credible limitation that must be addressed. Some people have roles with complex contexts: multiple projects, multiple teams, multiple environments. They may need more categorisation than "home" and "work". Others may have accessibility needs or cognitive styles that benefit from more structure. In these cases, insisting on minimalism for its own sake can be unhelpful. The reconciliation is to keep the categories functional and stable even if there are more of them. The question is not how many categories exist, but whether they reduce searching and forgetting without creating a maintenance burden that undermines trust. If the categories are stable, memorable, and easy to apply, they can be more numerous without becoming a trap. If they are ambiguous, overlapping, or constantly changing, even a modest number will cause friction.

Another limitation is that categories can become an excuse to defer deciding what to do. People can spend time moving tasks between categories as a substitute for taking action, a form of list-tidying that feels productive. This is the cosmetic maintenance trap that will be addressed more directly in the next subchapter, but it matters here because categories can feed it. The reconciliation is to remember what categorisation is for: to make tasks findable at the moment they can be done, not to provide the sensation of control through endless rearrangement. If you find yourself repeatedly reclassifying tasks, the problem is likely not the category system but the tasks themselves: they may be blur tasks without clear next actions, or they may be projects masquerading as tasks.

The quiet motif for this subchapter is the signpost. A signpost is not the territory. It is a pointer that helps you move. Too few signposts and you wander. Too many and you stop to read them all, losing time and confidence. The best signpost is obvious in the moment it is needed and invisible the rest of the time. That is what simple categories can become: a small set of pointers that allow you to act without searching, and to trust that you will not forget what matters because it has a home.

The forward test is therefore practical rather than ideological. When you are tired, rushed, and trying to choose what to do next, do your categories help you move, or do they demand a second round of thinking before you even begin?

Reviewing without rewriting

In April 1970 in Houston, Texas, Mission Control faced a situation in which rewriting the plan endlessly would have been a kind of theatre. Apollo 13 had suffered a catastrophic failure, and every hour required clarity, not aesthetic order. Teams gathered information, checked it against constraints, made decisions, and translated those decisions into actions. The work was messy. It was also effective. Nobody won awards for tidy notes. They were trying to get people home. The lesson is uncomfortable for anyone who finds comfort in organisation: sometimes the desire to make things look clean is the enemy of making things work.

Tidiness can be a delay tactic.

Most people do not rewrite their task lists because they are vain. They rewrite because rewriting creates a sensation of control without demanding the discomfort of commitment. A person opens their list, feels the pressure of what is pending, and responds by rearranging. They move items into new categories, rewrite phrasing, reorder priorities, add tags, delete and re-add, chase the feeling that if the list were just a bit neater, action would become easy. The feeling is briefly soothing. The list looks better. The week does not. The open loops remain open, only now with improved typography.

The central tension is between review as decision-making and review as self-soothing. Review that produces decisions reduces attention leakage. Review that produces cosmetic change often increases it, because it keeps tasks alive without moving them forward. The mind is not fooled for long. It can tell the difference between a list that has been refined and a life that has been stabilised. This is why people can spend an hour "getting organised" and still feel no lighter. They have performed maintenance on the representation of their work, not on the work's actual state.

A scene from an ordinary Sunday reset hour shows how rewriting seduces. Someone sits down with a clear intention to prepare the week. They open their list and immediately see blur tasks, half-finished items, and projects masquerading as tasks. Rather than confronting the discomfort of deciding what matters and what will happen next, they start polishing. They rewrite "sort finances" into "review finances" and then into "handle bank stuff". They add a tag. They create a new category called "admin". They move items around. The list becomes calmer to look at, but nothing has been decided. They have not scheduled the appointment. They have not sent the follow-up. They have not deleted the item that is no longer relevant. The concept here is representational work versus state-change work. The implication is blunt: only state changes reduce the ping.

This matters because rewriting is a particularly efficient way to avoid emotional friction. Many tasks are avoided not because they are difficult, but because they carry discomfort: uncertainty, social awkwardness, fear of discovering bad news, the need to make a trade-off, the risk of being wrong. Rewriting allows the person to touch the task without touching its discomfort. It is a way of staying near the problem without entering it. The mind experiences proximity as progress for a moment, then realises nothing has shifted and pings again. This is how people get trapped in cycles of constant list management. They do not trust their system because the system has become a place where tasks can be endlessly handled without being handled.

Psychology offers a useful lens for why this pattern is so persistent. People often substitute an easier action for a harder one when under cognitive or emotional load. Kahneman's work on fast and slow thinking describes how the mind defaults to easier operations when it is strained (Kahneman, 2011). Rewriting is easier than deciding, because deciding commits you to an outcome and exposes you to the consequences. Rewriting allows you to postpone consequences while still feeling active. The implication for the Sunday reset is that a review that invites endless rewriting is structurally vulnerable. It creates the conditions for substitution, and substitution is how the urgent and the cosmetic steal the hour.

There is another mechanism at work: the sunk cost effect. Once someone has spent time improving the list, they feel compelled to keep improving it to justify the effort. Arkes and Blumer described how people can continue an endeavour because of prior investment rather than current value (Arkes and Blumer, 1985). In a task system, this looks like "I have already reorganised half the list, so I might as well finish reorganising it." The week does not care. The calendar does not care. The only thing that changes is how long the person stays trapped in representational work. The implication is that rewriting can become self-perpetuating. It consumes the time that would have been used for the decisions that actually reduce stress.

Reviewing without rewriting requires a different definition of what a review is for. A review is not a makeover. It is a scan for status, followed by a small number of decisive interventions. Status means: is this done, is it scheduled, is it delegated, is it waiting, is it obsolete, is it a project that needs parking, is it a blur task that needs a clear next action. Intervention means a state change: a calendar entry created, a message sent, a task deleted, a follow-up queued, a project placed into a separate plan. These interventions can be quick. They can also be uncomfortable. That discomfort is the signal that the review is touching reality rather than the list's appearance.

The distinction becomes clearer if you watch your own behaviour. Rewriting produces longer lists with smoother phrasing and more elaborate categories. It tends to increase the number of words per task while reducing the number of commitments on the calendar. Decision-based review produces the opposite pattern. The list may remain a little rough, but the week becomes more stable. A handful of items disappear because they are deleted or completed. Others become runnable because they are rewritten into clear next actions, not polished descriptions. A few are scheduled, which moves them out of the list and into time. The implication is that the real output of a review is not a prettier list. It is a calendar that holds, a shortlist that can be completed, and fewer open loops.

A second named, checkable example from organisational practice reinforces why this matters. In October 2012, GOV.UK's consolidation approach was not primarily about rewriting content to sound better; it was about reducing duplication and making pathways reliable. The work that mattered was not cosmetic. It was structural. A personal task system is similar. You can rephrase tasks endlessly, but if your commitments remain scattered across tools, or your projects remain misclassified, or your calendar does not reflect reality, the system remains unreliable. Reliability is what reduces monitoring. Monitoring is what exhausts you.

There is a credible limitation, and it needs to be admitted to prevent the argument becoming puritanical. Sometimes rewriting is necessary. If tasks are unclear, rewriting them into clear next actions is valuable work. If categories are chaotic, simplifying them can reduce future friction. If the system has accumulated cruft, a brief clean-up can restore trust. The issue is not any rewriting. The issue is *endless* rewriting that does not create state changes. The reconciliation is to treat rewriting as surgery, not grooming: do it when it removes a blockage, stop when the blockage is removed. A surgeon does not keep cutting because the incision could be prettier. They close the loop and move on.

Another limitation is aesthetic. Some people genuinely think better when their external environment is orderly, including their lists. A bit of tidying can reduce cognitive noise for them. That is valid. The danger is when tidying becomes the substitute for acting, and the person starts to measure their week by the elegance of their system rather than by the stability of their commitments. The metric, again, is behavioural. If the tidy list leads to less checking and more follow-through, it is serving you. If it leads to more time spent maintaining the list, it has become the master.

The motif for this subchapter is the polish. Polish can make an object attractive. It cannot make an object structurally sound. A chair with glossy varnish still collapses if its joints are loose. A task list with beautiful categories still fails if it does not produce clear next actions and stable scheduling. The Sunday reset is not a craft session for polishing the list. It is a maintenance ritual for tightening joints: deciding, scheduling, delegating, deleting, and parking.

The forward test is therefore uncomfortable and clean. When you feel the urge to rewrite your list, what are you avoiding: an unclear next action, an unmade decision, a task that should be deleted, or a commitment that belongs on the calendar rather than on the list?

Chapter 8
Household preparation in 15 minutes

A Monday morning can collapse on something absurdly small. The keys are not where they should be. A uniform is damp. The lunch plan is a blank. A bag is half packed with yesterday's debris. Someone asks what is for dinner, and the question lands like an accusation because it is really five questions at once: what do we have, what needs using, who will be home, how much time is there, what will everyone tolerate. None of these problems is catastrophic. That is why they are dangerous. They repeat. They drain. They turn ordinary mornings into a series of tiny emergencies that make the week feel harder than it needs to.

Another household looks tidy enough and still bleeds time. Surfaces collect objects that do not belong there. Laundry exists in limbo, neither clean nor wearable. Food basics run out at inconvenient moments. The home becomes a place where small decisions are constantly required: where is the thing, what should I do with this, what is the plan. These decisions are rarely noted in calendars or task lists, yet they consume attention just as surely as work obligations. People often blame themselves for being scattered when the environment is asking for constant micro-decisions. The home becomes a decision factory.

Friction is the real enemy.

That is the central tension of household preparation. The week is not derailed by one big event. It is eroded by repeated small frictions that multiply stress and steal attention from everything else. A household reset is not about domestic virtue or aesthetic perfection. It is about reducing the number of times you have to think about the same basic logistical questions, especially when you are tired, rushed, or trying to get out of the door. The home is not separate from the Sunday reset. It is part of the system. If the household is not prepared in small but strategic ways, the rest of the week is forced to compensate through improvisation, and improvisation is expensive.

The trade-off here is between ambition and sustainability. Many people respond to household overwhelm by imagining a dramatic overhaul: deep cleaning, full decluttering, perfect meal planning, the kind of Sunday that looks impressive and feels punishing. That approach usually fails not because the person lacks commitment but because it demands too much time and emotional labour. The failure then becomes evidence that the household cannot be managed, which encourages avoidance, which allows friction to accumulate. The alternative is less glamorous and more effective: a short routine aimed at the friction points that affect the whole week. It accepts that a home is a living system, not a project to be completed.

The stakes are immediate because household friction has a unique talent for contaminating other domains. A morning made chaotic by missing items and unmade decisions does not only cost minutes. It changes the emotional tone of the day. People begin tense. They communicate more sharply. They arrive at work or school already depleted. The mind then has less capacity for the tasks that require thought, which produces a second layer of stress later. Household preparation is therefore not merely "domestic". It is a way of protecting attention and relationships by reducing predictable points of irritation. When the basics are handled, the week begins with less noise.

The longer-term stakes are about self-trust. When the household regularly causes avoidable friction, people start to treat the week as inherently unstable. They stop making plans because plans feel fragile. They become reactive, living from one micro-crisis to the next. A small household reset reverses this not by creating perfection but by creating reliability. Reliability is visible. It shows up as fewer last-minute searches, fewer rushed departures, fewer nights when dinner becomes a desperate improvisation, fewer moments of silent resentment at the amount of invisible work required to keep life moving. Reliability is not a personality trait. It is an outcome of repeated small design choices.

The motif for this chapter is the doorway. The doorway is where mornings succeed or fail. It is where bags are grabbed, shoes searched for, keys located, permission slips remembered, and the first anxious question of the day often arrives: are we ready. A doorway can either be a choke point or a launch point. The difference is rarely decor. It is whether the basics are in place and whether the decisions have been made in advance. A home reset is, in part, a decision to move certain choices away from the doorway and into a calmer moment.

The path here begins with the home basics that create disproportionate friction when neglected: the flows that determine whether everyday life feels smooth or sticky. It then turns towards a deliberately modest form of readiness for Monday, not as a full household transformation but as the preparation of a few high-impact items that reduce morning decision-making. The emphasis remains on selectivity. A small number of actions, chosen well, can change the week far more than an ambitious overhaul that collapses under its own weight.

The unresolved friction that pulls us into the practical work is not about cleanliness. It is about repeatable stress. Which small household failure point keeps stealing your Monday, not because it is hard, but because it is never handled at a time when handling it is easy?

Resetting the home basics

In Frankfurt am Main in 1926, the architect Margarete Schuette-Lihotzky designed what became known as the Frankfurt Kitchen, a compact domestic workspace intended to reduce wasted movement and make everyday tasks less draining (Schuette-Lihotzky, 1926). It was not a lifestyle fantasy. It was an attempt to treat the home as a system with friction points, where small design decisions could remove recurring strain. The kitchen did not promise beauty. It promised flow. The premise still matters. Most household stress is not caused by rare disasters; it is caused by ordinary repetition.

The home is a machine of micro-decisions. Where are the clean clothes. What is for dinner. Where did the paperwork go. Which surface is usable. Each question is small. Each question is also a demand on attention. When the answers are not ready, the questions multiply and appear at the worst times, usually when someone is rushing out of the door or too tired to think clearly. The result is a week that feels louder than it should, not because it contains more responsibilities than other weeks, but because the household keeps calling for fresh decisions.

Small resets change everything.

The central idea of a home basics reset is not cleanliness as virtue. It is friction reduction. Friction is the moment where life should move and instead catches. A drawer that jams. A laundry pile that cannot be classified into clean or dirty. A fridge that offers ingredients but no plan. A counter that has become a storage shelf, leaving nowhere to place the next thing. Each friction point forces a decision, a search, or an improvisation. Those actions are not recorded in most task systems, which is why household strain can feel invisible and therefore strangely inexhaustible. The reset does not aim to do all the work. It aims to stop the work from being constantly re-created.

A quick surface clear illustrates how small friction becomes daily taxation. Imagine the end of a weekday evening. A person wants to make tea, answer a message, perhaps pack a lunch. They approach the kitchen counter and find it covered with objects that do not belong together: post, receipts, chargers, a half-empty bag, yesterday's mug, a school note, a bottle that needs returning. Nothing here is dramatic. Yet each object is a question: keep, bin, move, file, wash. The counter is no longer a work surface; it is a decision surface. The concept is decision load. The implication is immediate: when a key surface is occupied, the household forces repeated micro-decisions, and micro-decisions make people feel as if they are always behind.

This is why the reset targets "key surfaces" rather than the whole house. Key surfaces are the points where life passes through: kitchen counter, dining table edge, entryway, bedside. These places are not morally important. They are functionally important. When they are clogged, they generate searching, shifting, and irritation. When they are clear enough, the home becomes easier to use. The phrase "clear enough" matters. It frees the reset from perfectionism. A surface does not need to look like a showroom. It needs to behave like a tool. Tool surfaces should be usable at speed.

The same logic applies to laundry, which many people experience as an endless moral failing rather than a simple flow problem. Laundry becomes stressful when it lives in limbo: piles that are neither dirty nor clean, clean items that are not wearable because they are not where they should be, missing essentials discovered only when it is too late. The visible behaviour is familiar: morning searches, emergency washes, last-minute substitutions that irritate everyone, and that low-level dread when you think about the state of the pile. The name for what is missing is not "motivation". It is a reliable sequence: dirty to basket, basket to wash, wash to dry, dry to wearable storage. When the sequence breaks at one point, the whole system feels impossible. The implication is that a laundry reset is not "do all the laundry". It is restore the flow so the week stops producing avoidable surprises.

Food basics are a similarly potent friction point because they sit at the intersection of energy, time, and mood. The question "what are we eating" becomes hard when the fridge contains ingredients but no readiness: nothing defrosted, nothing obvious, no staples that allow a quick default. When defaults are missing, every meal becomes a negotiation and a planning task, which is a cruel demand at the end of a long day. The concept here is choice architecture, a term often used in behavioural economics to describe how environments shape decisions (Thaler and Sunstein, 2008). The home version is not policy. It is practical: if basic options are not prepared, the household demands complex decision-making at low-energy times. The implication is that a small reset aimed at food basics is not about culinary ambition; it is about reducing evening decision load.

A second checkable historical example helps because it shows that household "systems thinking" is not new, and not a fad. In New York in 1919, Christine Frederick published *Household Engineering: Scientific Management in the Home*, applying time-and-motion logic to domestic work (Frederick, 1919). The book reflects its era, and modern readers may rightly bristle at some of its assumptions, yet the underlying observation is still useful: repetitive tasks become bearable when their steps are simplified, and unbearable when they are repeatedly reinvented. The aim is not to treat a home like a factory. The aim is to notice where repeated reinvention is quietly stealing time and attention.

These three targets, surfaces, laundry flow, and food basics, share a structural property: they are upstream. They shape many later moments. A clear counter makes cooking and packing easier. A laundry flow prevents emergency mornings.

Food basics reduce negotiation and late shopping. In systems terms, upstream interventions have downstream benefits. The behavioural metrics are straightforward. Fewer frantic searches for essential items. Fewer moments when you cannot start a task because there is nowhere to put things. Fewer evenings where dinner becomes a stressful improvisation. Fewer household arguments that are not really arguments, but exhaustion expressed through irritation.

A reset also has to respect the reality that households are shared systems. One person can do heroic work and still fail to reduce friction if the household has no stable "places" for things or no shared understanding of the basic flow. The result is a familiar pattern: surfaces are cleared and immediately re-cluttered, laundry is washed and immediately scattered, food is planned and immediately disrupted by unknown preferences and last-minute changes. The concept here is shared defaults. The implication is not that everyone must agree on everything. It is that small defaults, like a designated place for keys, a consistent laundry basket location, or a known set of staple foods, reduce conflict because they reduce decision-making at high-stress times. When defaults exist, people do not need to negotiate basic logistics repeatedly.

This is also where the Sunday reset's wider discipline matters: boundaries. A home basics reset is intentionally small because its purpose is leverage, not labour. When people attempt to overhaul the whole house, the session expands, fatigue rises, and the practice becomes unsustainable. The week then begins without any reset at all, which is worse than a modest one. A home basics reset that fits is closer to triage than to transformation. It asks a blunt question: which friction points will most reliably steal time and patience during the week if they are left untouched?

A credible limitation should be admitted, because not all homes can be made frictionless in a meaningful sense. Small spaces, shared living arrangements, limited storage, unpredictable care demands, or periods of illness can make even the basics feel hard. In such contexts, aiming for a full "reset" can feel like a joke, and that feeling can become a reason to do nothing. The reconciliation is to tighten the definition of success. The goal is not an orderly home. The goal is a home that produces fewer avoidable micro-emergencies. Even when the environment is constrained, one or two friction points can often be eased. The strategy shifts from "make it nice" to "make it usable". Usability is more forgiving and more realistic.

Another limitation is psychological. Some people use household tasks as a way to avoid deeper work that requires concentration or emotional courage. Clearing surfaces can become a comforting ritual that substitutes for harder choices. This does not make household care meaningless. It simply means the home basics reset must remain bounded and purposeful. Its place in the Sunday reset is to remove friction that would otherwise sabotage the week, not to become a whole Sunday activity dressed up as responsibility. The measure is again behavioural: does the reset lead to smoother weekdays, or does it merely provide temporary relief while larger priorities remain untouched?

The motif that unifies this subchapter is the countertop. Not as an aesthetic symbol, but as a test of usability. A usable counter suggests a household that is not constantly improvising. An unusable counter suggests a household that is storing decisions in physical form. When you clear a counter, you are not merely moving objects. You are closing questions. You are saying, this belongs here, this belongs there, this leaves the house, this can be binned. In that sense, household preparation is a form of closure, and closure is what quietens the mind.

The forward test is therefore deliberately simple. When you imagine your next Monday, what is the first small household friction that reliably turns into stress, and what would change if that one friction point were made *clear enough* on Sunday for the week to move without catching?

Creating a "Monday ready" setup

In 1960 in Cambridge, Massachusetts, the psychologist George A. Miller published work that became famous for discussing limits in what people can hold in mind at once (Miller, 1956). The paper is often reduced to a slogan, but its practical implication is older than psychology and visible in every rushed morning: when too many small decisions are required at speed, errors rise. People forget. They improvise. They become irritable. A Monday morning is a decision storm, and storms punish systems that rely on memory and last-minute judgement.

Monday is unforgiving.

It is not that Monday is uniquely tragic. It is that Monday is the point where the week's abstract intentions become concrete actions under time pressure. The first day often carries transitions: back to work, back to school runs, back to routines that were loosened over the weekend. The mind is shifting gears. The body is adjusting. In that state, small points of friction take on disproportionate power. A missing key document, a bag half-packed, a uniform discovered to be unwearable, a meal plan that is still a question rather than a decision. Each missing piece triggers a micro-scramble, and micro-scrambles stack. The day begins in reaction, and that reactive tone spreads into everything that follows.

A "Monday ready" setup is a way of taking those micro-scrambles out of the morning and placing them into a calmer moment. It is not a domestic performance. It is risk reduction. The risk is not only that something is forgotten. The risk is that the household starts the week already depleted, already annoyed, already behind. When the morning begins with searching, negotiating, and inventing, the mind spends its best attention on logistics rather than on the work and relationships that actually matter. A small setup shifts the allocation of attention. It protects the morning's limited clarity for things that cannot be done the night before.

A scene makes the logic obvious. Imagine a household where Monday begins with a search: where is the permission slip, where are the shoes, where is the charging cable, where is the badge, where is the lunch box. Each search creates a second problem. A drawer is opened and left open. A pile is disturbed. A person interrupts another person. Voices rise. Time becomes the villain. The household is not failing morally. It is operating without a staging area. Staging areas are how complex systems move smoothly: items are gathered, checked, and placed where they will be needed. Without staging, the system relies on frantic recall. Recall is unreliable under stress.

This is why "Monday ready" is about choosing one or two high-impact preparations rather than attempting to overhaul the entire home. Overhaul is seductive because it promises that if everything were finally sorted, mornings would be calm forever. The promise is counterfeit. Homes are living systems. They produce mess as a by-product of life. Overhaul creates fatigue and resentment, which makes it unlikely to be repeated, and a ritual that cannot be repeated will not protect the week. High-impact preparation, by contrast, is modest and targeted. It accepts that you cannot eliminate all friction, but you can remove the friction that reliably causes the most damage at the start of the week. The implication is simple: selectivity is the skill, not intensity.

A useful concept here is cognitive offloading, the practice of moving information out of the mind into the environment so it does not need to be remembered in the moment. Research in cognitive psychology has examined how people use external tools and the environment to support memory and action, from notes to physical placement of objects (see, for example,

Risko and Gilbert, 2016, on cognitive offloading). Again, the point is not to turn your hallway into a laboratory. The point is that placing a bag by the door is not mere tidiness. It is an external memory cue. Packing a uniform the night before is not an aesthetic choice. It is offloading. The environment becomes a collaborator. When the environment collaborates, the mind does not have to carry everything.

This is also where the earlier theme of trust returns. A "Monday ready" setup works when the household learns that certain items will be where they should be. That learning reduces monitoring. People stop doing repeated checks because they have evidence. Evidence is more soothing than intention. When the setup is inconsistent, the mind compensates by checking anyway: checking the bag, checking the uniform, checking the documents, checking the fridge. Those checks are a symptom of mistrust, and mistrust is a form of attention leakage. A consistent setup turns checking into a single glance or removes the need for it altogether.

The "simple plan for meals" is often misunderstood in this context. It is not about culinary ambition or nutrition debates. It is about decision load. Meal questions tend to arrive at the end of the day, when attention is depleted. Without a plan, the household must decide under low energy, which increases conflict and reduces satisfaction. The plan does not need to be elaborate. It needs to exist. Existence is the key. A decided default is kinder than repeated negotiation. This is why preparation focuses on what removes the most repeated decisions: not every meal, not every day, but the points where the household routinely stalls and then pays for that stall in stress.

A second checkable example from design history reinforces why staging matters. The Frankfurt Kitchen was intended to reduce unnecessary movement and streamline repetitive domestic work by placing tools and supplies where they are used (Schuette-Lihotzky, 1926). The modern home does not need to mimic its aesthetics to learn from its intent: reduce friction by bringing the next required item closer to the point of action. A "Monday ready" setup is the temporal version of this. It places what Monday needs closer to Monday, by shifting it into Sunday evening or another calm time. The implication is that preparation is not about doing more. It is about doing certain small tasks at a better time.

A credible limitation should be faced, because not all households can prepare Monday in the same way. Some people live in shared spaces without much control over surfaces. Some have fluctuating schedules and uncertain Monday demands. Some have care situations that make evenings chaotic. In those contexts, the ideal of a calm pre-Monday ritual can feel unrealistic. The reconciliation is to keep the principle while shrinking the scope: identify what causes the worst morning friction and move only that. The principle is not "prepare everything". The principle is "reduce the most expensive searches and decisions". Even one moved decision can change the morning's tone.

Another limitation is psychological. Preparation can slide into anxiety. Some people cope with uncertainty by over-preparing, packing for every scenario, creating complicated check routines that consume time and create tension if disturbed. In such cases, "Monday ready" can become another performance. The aim remains modest: a few stabilising moves that reduce friction without turning Sunday evening into a rehearsal for catastrophe. A system that is too complex becomes fragile. Fragile systems invite checking. Checking invites resentment. The cycle returns.

The quiet motif for this subchapter is the launch pad. A launch pad is not the whole journey. It is the place where you begin without stumbling. A bag by the door is a launch pad. A uniform laid out is a launch pad. A document placed in the right spot is a launch pad. A simple meal decision made ahead is a launch pad. Launch pads reduce tripping. They do not guarantee a smooth day, but they change the first few minutes, and the first few minutes often decide the emotional weather of the whole day.

The forward test is therefore not whether you can prepare perfectly. It is whether you can identify the one or two recurring points where Monday routinely trips you and move them onto the launch pad, so that the week begins with fewer searches, fewer negotiations, and fewer avoidable scrambles.

Chapter 9
Money and admin quick checks

A letter lands on the mat and nobody picks it up. It is not dramatic. It is an envelope with a logo, a windowed address, a tone that suggests obligation. It sits there for a day, then two, then becomes part of the scenery. Another message arrives by email with a subject line that feels heavy: renewal, payment, confirmation needed. The person reads enough to feel the tug and then closes it because there is no time to deal with it properly. The week continues. The mind does not. It keeps a quiet tally of what has not been identified, and that tally produces a low-level dread that is out of proportion to the actual work involved.

Later, a small surprise appears. A charge was larger than expected. A balance is lower than it should be. A deadline is closer than remembered. The surprise does not only cost money or time. It costs composure. It turns a routine evening into a scramble, because scrambles are what happen when admin is discovered late. People then tell themselves they must become "better with money" or "more organised", as if the problem were a personality trait. Often the problem is simpler: there was no regular, bounded moment to look.

Avoidance feeds uncertainty.

That is the central tension of money and admin. These domains are emotionally charged for many people, not because they are inherently complicated but because they carry consequences and shame, and shame makes attention slippery. When something is even slightly uncomfortable, the mind finds reasons to postpone it, and postponement allows uncertainty to grow. Uncertainty is what creates dread. Paperwork becomes frightening when it is unidentified. Account checks become threatening when they are avoided for long enough that any glance might reveal a problem. Renewals become ambushes when they are not placed into a system that remembers on your behalf. The aim here is not to achieve mastery or optimisation. The aim is to reduce the uncertainty that turns small admin into a source of constant background stress.

The stakes are immediate because money and admin are domains where small delays can cascade. A missed payment leads to a chain of follow-ups. An unreturned form blocks another process. An ignored message creates a social friction that grows as time passes. Even when the consequences are minor, the psychological cost can be large because the mind treats uninspected obligations as potential threats. The result is repeated checking without resolution: opening and closing the same email, thinking about the same bill while doing something else, promising yourself you will "sort it" later. The Sunday reset is designed to stop this kind of mental pinging by giving it a designated container and a deliberate, time-limited response.

The longer-term stakes are about trust in your own life. When money and admin are handled only in emergencies, a person starts to treat their week as a trap: a place where surprises are waiting. This breeds hypervigilance, which is exhausting, or denial, which is risky. A quick weekly check changes the relationship. It does not promise that nothing unexpected will happen. It promises that unexpected things are more likely to be noticed early, when options are wider and emotions are calmer. That is control in the sense this book has been using all along: fewer avoidable alarms.

The danger is to turn this into an elaborate budgeting exercise or a full administrative overhaul, which would be unsustainable for most people and would quickly become another avoided ritual. The power of a quick check is its modesty. It aims for awareness, not perfection. Awareness means seeing what is coming, noticing what is odd, and converting dread into a small number of concrete next actions. That conversion is the key. Without it, a check becomes a worry session. With it, a check becomes a stabilising practice that reduces mental noise rather than increasing it.

The motif for this chapter is the unopened drawer. An unopened drawer can hold anything: lost documents, forgotten obligations, harmless clutter, or something that needs action. The uncertainty is what makes it unpleasant to open. Many people treat their accounts, their paperwork, and their admin messages like unopened drawers, not because they are careless, but because they fear what they might find and they have no bounded time to deal with it if the find is difficult. A weekly quick check is the act of opening the drawer when you have chosen to do so, so that the contents stop haunting you in imagination.

The path here begins with a brief scan that catches upcoming payments, low balances, and anything unexpected before it becomes a scramble. It then turns to the piles and inboxes where paper and messages accumulate, using a simple triage that forces identification and creates a short list rather than a fog of dread. It ends by gathering the recurring tasks that otherwise ambush you, not by trying to remember them, but by placing them into a system that will prompt you at the right moment, so they stop occupying mental space.

The unresolved friction that pulls us into the practical work is both ordinary and revealing. When you think about money and admin, what do you avoid looking at because it feels heavier than it probably is, and what would change if you gave it a small, regular moment of attention before it becomes urgent?

Scanning accounts and bills

In Venice in 1494, the Franciscan friar Luca Pacioli published *Summa de arithmetica, geometria, proportioni et proportionalita,* a compendium that included a clear description of double-entry bookkeeping. The setting is easy to romanticise: ink, ledgers, merchants, the damp tang of a port city. Yet the idea itself is almost brutally modern. It treats financial life as something that can be observed, recorded, and reconciled, rather than as a series of shocks endured in real time. It assumes that if the books are not looked at, the mind will fill the silence with anxiety or fantasy.

Surprise is expensive in life.

Most people do not fear money because they are incapable of arithmetic. They fear money because money is where consequences hide: a payment that arrives unexpectedly, a balance that is lower than assumed, a bill that was "surely already handled", a charge that looks unfamiliar, a renewal that lands at the wrong moment. The dread is often less about the amount and more about the feeling of being caught unprepared. And because that feeling is unpleasant, many people postpone looking. Postponement does not remove the risk. It concentrates it.

A brief scan changes the emotional geometry of the week because it replaces suspense with information. The key word is *brief*. This is not a demand for detailed budgeting, forensic analysis, or heroic financial self-improvement. It is an awareness practice with practical edges: notice what is due, notice what is odd, notice what would cause a scramble if discovered late. In other words, reduce uncertainty. Uncertainty is what triggers the mental pinging described earlier in the book. When the status of something important is unknown, the mind monitors. Monitoring steals attention. A small scan, done regularly, gives the mind permission to stop patrolling.

The first claim is simple: the brain treats unseen obligations as potential threats, and threat is sticky. A person who has not looked at their account for a while may experience a low-grade unease that appears at odd moments. It surfaces when they consider making a purchase, when they open the post, when they see a notification from a service provider, when someone suggests a plan for the week. Even if nothing is wrong, the *not knowing* occupies space. This is not moral weakness. It is a response to uncertainty with real-world consequences. When the mind cannot estimate the risk, it assumes the risk might be high. That assumption is cognitively expensive.

A second claim is that avoidance makes even routine admin feel heavier than it is. Paperwork and payments have a peculiar property: they grow in imagination. A bill left unopened becomes, in the mind, a symbol of everything one does not want to face. An account not checked becomes a dark room where anything might be waiting. This is why the first glance can feel hard. It is not simply "doing admin". It is collapsing a cloud of imagined possibilities into a set of facts. Facts can be handled. Clouds cannot. The implication is that the scan is not primarily about money; it is about turning unknowns into knowns so attention stops leaking into worry.

The scan is also a defence against a particular cognitive bias: once a week begins, people tend to anchor their sense of financial and administrative reality to what they last remember, not to what is currently true. That remembered picture may be accurate. It may not. Either way, it becomes the reference point for decisions, and decisions made from stale reference points are more likely to require later correction. Behavioural economics has made popular the idea that people use mental shortcuts under uncertainty, and Kahneman's work on judgement and decision-making describes how quick intuitions often dominate unless deliberate checks are built into a process (Kahneman, 2011). The implication here is not that everyone is irrational. It is that systems that rely on "I think it's fine" will occasionally be wrong, and the cost of being wrong lands at inconvenient times.

A third claim is that a scan is valuable because it produces *early detection*, not because it produces perfection. Early detection changes what options are available. When something is noticed early, there is room to plan calmly, to gather information, to decide what action is needed, and to schedule that action. When something is noticed late, it becomes a scramble, and scrambles tend to cost more than the original issue because they consume time, attention, and emotional composure. This is where "efficiency" becomes a humane concept: not speed, but reduced emergency labour. An efficient week is one with fewer avoidable scrambles.

Two named moments outside the domestic sphere sharpen why early detection matters. On 15 September 2008 in New York City, Lehman Brothers filed for bankruptcy, a visible marker in the global financial crisis. For many people, the lived experience of that period was not an abstract economic narrative but a series of sudden changes: credit tightening, job insecurity, institutions behaving unpredictably. The lesson, in miniature, is that systems can shift quickly, and what felt stable last month may not be stable now. A weekly scan does not prevent systemic events. It prevents the additional suffering of being the last to notice changes in one's own accounts and obligations. It is a small personal habit built for a world where not everything is predictable.

The other anchor returns us to the older world of ledgers, because the concept is timeless. Pacioli's contribution was not merely a technique; it was a discipline of reconciliation. Reconciliation means comparing what you think is true to what is recorded as true, and then resolving discrepancies. The word matters. It implies an end to argument. A weekly scan is a reconciliation ritual in miniature. It asks, quietly, whether the week ahead contains any hidden clashes: payments due, renewals approaching, balances that might not support planned outgoings, charges that require explanation. It does not solve everything. It makes the status visible.

A scan also makes clear the difference between *awareness* and *control*. Awareness means seeing what is coming and what is odd. Control, in the deeper sense, means reducing attention leakage by giving those observations a place to go: a note, a reminder, a scheduled admin action, a question to resolve later. The trap is to confuse awareness with immediate action. Some people avoid looking because they fear that once they look they will have to fix everything at once. That fear is rational if past experiences have turned "checking" into a rabbit hole. The discipline of this book is containment. The scan is bounded. Its job is to surface what needs attention, not to become an entire budgeting session.

This is why the scan is best understood as a *dashboard glance*. A driver does not dismantle the engine every time a warning light appears. They notice the light, interpret what it likely signifies, and decide what action is needed and when. The dashboard glance does not deny complexity. It prevents surprise. A personal money-and-bills scan is a dashboard glance: look for the equivalents of warning lights. Upcoming obligations. Unexpected charges. A pattern that seems off. A balance that suggests an oncoming squeeze. The dashboard motif matters because it keeps the practice psychologically manageable. It frames the scan as normal monitoring, not as a moral reckoning.

The scan also interacts with time in a subtle way. Many payments and bills are time-bound even when the amounts are not the central concern. Time-bound obligations produce urgency if ignored, and urgency is the kind of pressure that hijacks weeks. The scan therefore functions as an anti-panic measure. It brings forward the moment of awareness, which allows the rest of the Sunday reset to do its work: convert anxiety into decisions and place those decisions into calendars and task lists. An item seen early can be parked or scheduled. An item seen late demands immediate attention and steals from higher-value work.

A counter-example is important here, because the scan can be misused. For some people, frequent checking becomes compulsive and increases anxiety rather than reducing it. The dashboard becomes something they stare at constantly, hunting for danger, interpreting every fluctuation as a threat. In such cases, the problem is not the absence of information but the relationship to uncertainty. The reconciliation is to return to the principle of containment. The scan is not meant to provide constant reassurance. It is meant to provide periodic clarity. Clarity has a rhythm. Too little produces surprise. Too much produces rumination. The Sunday reset is designed to set that rhythm: one deliberate check that feeds decisions, rather than many anxious checks that feed worry.

Another limitation is structural. Some people's financial lives involve genuine complexity: irregular income, shared accounts, multiple currencies, or administrative systems that are opaque and slow. In such contexts, a simple scan may not yield simple answers, and the scan might surface questions that cannot be resolved quickly. This does not make the scan useless. It makes its role even more valuable. When complexity exists, the worst outcome is to leave it uninspected until it becomes urgent. The scan does not simplify the world. It allows you to see the world you are in. Seeing is the precondition for any calm response.

What, then, counts as "unexpected" in a scan, and why does unexpectedness matter so much? Unexpectedness is not only about a charge that you do not recognise. It is about any deviation from what you believed the week would require. The mind is constantly running a quiet prediction model: this is what I have, this is what I owe, this is what I can afford in time and attention. When reality violates the model, stress spikes. A scan updates the model. Updated models produce calmer decisions. This is why a scan that finds nothing unusual can still be valuable: it provides evidence that the model is accurate, and evidence reduces monitoring. A mind that trusts its model checks less often.

The scan also reduces the cognitive overhead of financial admin by narrowing where attention is directed. Without a scan, people often carry a vague sense of "I should look at that" for days, which is a kind of mental debt. With a scan, the concern becomes either resolved or turned into a specific follow-up action. Specificity is the friend of follow-through. It is the same principle seen throughout the book: open loops quieten when their next state is clear. A scan that leads to a clear note such as "confirm what this charge is" or "move this payment date into the calendar" is not yet a solution, but it is a containment move. Containment reduces mental noise.

The dashboard motif returns at the exact point where many people get stuck: the moment after noticing a warning light. There is a temptation to either panic and try to fix everything instantly, or to ignore the light entirely and hope it goes away. The middle path is to interpret and schedule. Some warning lights require immediate action. Many do not. A weekly scan is an educational practice precisely because it teaches judgement: what is actually time-sensitive, what is merely uncomfortable, what can wait, what requires a longer session, what should be delegated, what should be deleted as irrelevant worry. This judgement is not financial advice. It is life-admin literacy.

The unresolved tension that pulls this subchapter forward is simple and revealing. When a money-related worry appears in your mind midweek, is it pointing to a real upcoming obligation that would be calmer to see early, or is it pointing to the absence of a trusted dashboard glance that would let the mind stop imagining what might be hiding in the drawer?

Handling paperwork and messages

In April 1970 in Houston, Texas, Mission Control faced a constant flood of information: telemetry, calculations, warnings, instructions, confirmations. Apollo 13 demanded a discipline that looks, from a distance, almost dull. Incoming signals had to be identified, routed, and acted on in the right order. The danger was not only bad news. The danger was *unknown* news. An unidentified signal could not be ignored safely, and it could not be acted on intelligently. It had to be named first. Naming changed everything.

Unopened becomes unnerving.

Paperwork and important messages behave like unidentified signals. A letter on the mat is not just paper. It is an unknown that might contain a deadline, a request, a renewal, a charge, a correction, a mistake, or nothing of consequence at all. An email with a formal subject line is not just text. It is a potential obligation in hiding. When these items remain unidentified, the mind treats them as risks. Risk triggers monitoring. Monitoring feels like dread. The dread is often out of proportion to the actual task, but it is perfectly proportionate to uncertainty. A person can tolerate work. They struggle to tolerate not knowing what the work *is*.

A quick sort is therefore not clerical fussiness. It is an act of risk reduction and attention protection. It turns a pile of unknowns into a short list of knowns. That conversion is what removes the frightening quality. Paperwork becomes frightening when it is a fog. When it is named, it becomes bounded. Boundaries are calming because they allow you to decide. Decide is the operative verb. Much of the stress around paperwork is not caused by the work itself but by the repeated postponement of decision-making: repeated glances at the envelope, repeated scrolling past the email, repeated promises of "later". Later keeps the item alive as a background loop.

The triage method is blunt for a reason. Do, defer, delegate, delete. These are not motivational slogans. They are mutually exclusive states that a message or document must eventually enter if you want your attention back. The point of triage is not to handle everything immediately. The point is to decide what kind of handling is appropriate. When a document is triaged, it stops being a shapeless threat and becomes a thing with a fate. A fate can be uncomfortable. A lack of fate is worse.

A scene illustrates how triage prevents a common kind of self-sabotage. Someone opens a pile of post intending to "deal with it". The first letter is mildly complex. It requires a missing reference number. They feel a small spike of discomfort and put it aside. The second letter is a form. They skim, see it will take time, and put it aside. The third is a notification about something that might cost money. They do not want to look closely, so they put it aside. Ten minutes later, the pile has been rearranged. Nothing has been clarified. The person feels more stressed than when they started, because they have now confirmed their own suspicion that the pile is heavy. This is what happens when "dealing with paperwork" is treated as one amorphous task. The concept is avoidance by partial engagement. The implication is that partial engagement without classification increases dread, because it adds evidence of difficulty without producing closure.

Triage changes the structure of engagement. "Do" means an item can be completed quickly with what you have, and completion creates immediate closure. "Defer" means the item requires more time or information than you have in the moment, and deferral is only useful if it is explicit enough that it stops the mind from rethinking: what exactly is needed, and when will it be revisited. "Delegate" means the next action belongs to someone else, and delegation must be clear enough that ownership is transferred, not merely suggested. "Delete" means the item does not matter, is redundant, is spam, is a duplicate, or is no longer relevant, and deleting is a legitimate form of closure. Each state is a decision. Decisions reduce open loops.

This logic aligns with what has already been established about unfinished tasks and intrusive thoughts. Unfulfilled goals tend to linger, and research suggests that forming a plan can reduce intrusive thoughts about those goals (Masicampo and Baumeister, 2011). Triage is a micro-planning act. It assigns the next state. It prevents the mind from keeping the item warm. It also prevents the common behaviour of using the inbox or the letter pile as a reminder system, leaving items "unhandled" as a form of memory. That behaviour feels safe and is often unsafe, because it relies on constant rechecking and on the hope that nothing will slip under the pile.

A second named, checkable example outside domestic life shows why triage exists as a professional discipline. In emergency medicine, triage is used to allocate limited resources, deciding which cases must be handled immediately and which can safely wait. The term has a grim origin, but its logic can be used gently in everyday admin: not everything can be handled now, so decide what must be handled, what can be scheduled, what can be passed on, and what can be discarded. The personal value of triage is that it stops the endless internal argument about what to do with each item. The argument is draining. The decision is freeing.

Paperwork becomes frightening for another reason as well: it often carries ambiguous authority. Official-looking letters can feel like they come from an omniscient system that will punish mistakes. Even when the stakes are low, the tone can trigger stress. Important emails can carry similar weight, especially when they involve institutions, formal language, or potential consequences. The mind responds to perceived authority by becoming cautious, which slows action, which increases avoidance, which increases the pile. The pile then becomes a symbol of being behind in a domain where being behind feels dangerous. Triage cuts through this by refusing to treat the pile as a monolith. Each item is either actionable now, actionable later with a defined next step, actionable by someone else, or discardable. The pile loses its supernatural quality.

There is also an efficiency argument that is not about speed but about reducing rework. When items are not triaged, people repeatedly re-open them to re-interpret what they are. They read the first paragraph of the same email three times. They look at the envelope and try to remember whether it is urgent. They mentally reconstruct the task again and again. This is a form of cognitive switching, and research on task switching suggests that switching carries performance costs (Rubinstein, Meyer, and Evans, 2001). Triage reduces switching by ending interpretation. Once an item is classified, you do not need to keep re-reading it to decide what it is. You can move on. Moving on is the goal.

A quiet motif helps unify this subchapter: the label. Unlabelled boxes are unsettling because they force you to imagine what might be inside. Labelled boxes are less dramatic because they can be placed where they belong. Triage is labelling. It does not eliminate work. It eliminates the dread created by unlabelled obligations. When you label an item as "do", you create closure. When you label it as "defer", you create a container for later action. When you label it as "delegate", you create an ownership transfer. When you label it as "delete", you create release. The label is not decoration. It is a boundary.

A credible limitation needs to be respected. Some paperwork cannot be handled quickly, and some messages cannot be triaged without careful thought. Complex forms, sensitive correspondence, and anything involving legal or financial consequences may require more time than a weekly reset allows, and may require professional advice depending on the situation. The reconciliation is to keep the triage bounded and honest. The quick sort is not about completing complex matters. It is about identifying them and placing them into an appropriate next state so they stop living as unidentified threats. "Defer" is not a moral failure when it is explicit. It becomes a failure only when it is vague.

Another limitation is emotional. Some people use triage to delete discomfort rather than to manage it, discarding items that should be addressed because they fear conflict or consequence. This is human. It is also risky. The point of triage is not avoidance dressed as decisiveness. It is to align action with reality. Reality can include uncomfortable obligations.

The check is behavioural. Does triage reduce repeated rethinking and surprise emergencies, or does it produce new surprises later because important items were dismissed? A good triage system increases clarity, not denial.

Triage also benefits from being done in the right sequence within the Sunday reset. Capture brings items into one place. Review provides context. Decide assigns fates. Prepare schedules what must happen. Paperwork triage sits in this chain as a decisive moment: turn unidentified inputs into known categories, then ensure that what is deferred is truly parked in a way the week can hold. If triage is done without parking, deferred items simply become a new pile, and the mind resumes monitoring. The label must have a home.

The label motif returns at the end because it points to the forward test. When you look at your current paperwork pile or your "important" email backlog, how many items are frightening mainly because they are unlabelled, and what would change if each one were forced into a single fate: do, defer, delegate, or delete?

Renewals and recurring tasks

In 1758 in London, the Swedish botanist Carl Linnaeus published the tenth edition of *Systema Naturae*, a work that helped stabilise a way of naming and sorting living things so they could be recognised and managed rather than endlessly rediscovered. The content was scientific, but the underlying gesture was administrative: create a system that remembers, so the mind does not have to start from scratch each time. Without a system, each encounter feels like a surprise. With a system, recurrence becomes predictable.

Recurrence is not a surprise.

And yet recurring life tasks have a talent for arriving as ambush. A renewal pops up when you are already busy. A subscription charge appears when you thought you had cancelled it. An annual appointment comes due at a time that makes rescheduling difficult. A licence or policy needs updating when you have no spare attention. These events feel intrusive not because they are rare, but because they are *uncontained*. They live in a strange place between "known" and "forgotten". You know, abstractly, that some things recur. You do not know, concretely, when they will next demand action. The mind responds by keeping a background watch. That watch is tiring.

The central claim is simple: recurring tasks should not live in your head. They should live in a system that surfaces them at the right moment. "Right moment" matters. Too early and the reminder is ignored and then lost. Too late and the reminder becomes a scramble. The goal is not to build a perfect registry of every life obligation. The goal is to remove the most predictable ambushes by converting them into scheduled prompts. A prompt turns recurrence into a queue. Queues can be handled. Ambushes cannot.

A scene makes the mechanism familiar. Someone receives a renewal notice and feels a small spike of irritation. They put it aside. It is not urgent. Days pass. The notice disappears into a pile or into an email thread. Weeks later, the renewal becomes urgent because the window is closing or because a service depends on it. Now it is a crisis. The person must search for the notice, re-read details, perhaps find documents, perhaps make a call in a tight window. The real work has not changed much. The timing has. Timing is what creates stress. The concept here is administrative latency: the delay between when something becomes knowable and when it is acted on. The implication is that a system that reduces latency reduces stress, even if the underlying tasks remain the same.

Recurring tasks are particularly sticky because they blend into the "obvious" background of adulthood. The mind treats them as too mundane to deserve careful planning, which is why they are repeatedly reinvented. Each time, you have to remember the same facts, locate the same documents, repeat the same decisions. This is the hidden cost of not systematising recurrence. It is not only that you might miss something. It is that you repeatedly pay the set-up costs. If you have ever found yourself hunting for a policy number, searching for the last email from a provider, or trying to remember which month a renewal tends to land, you have felt those costs directly.

The discipline here is not complicated. It is classification and timing. Classification means recognising which tasks are recurring and naming them as such rather than treating them as one-off annoyances. Timing means placing a reminder not at the moment of panic but at a moment that allows calm action. This echoes a broader idea from human factors: systems should reduce reliance on memory for predictable events. In safety-critical domains, checklists and scheduled inspections exist precisely because people forget, not because people are negligent, but because memory is not designed to carry recurring obligations reliably under load. The personal version is less dramatic but structurally similar.

A checkable example helps because it shows how civil systems handle recurrence. Vehicle inspections, licence renewals, passport expiry, and similar administrative tasks are structured around formal renewal cycles and reminders in many jurisdictions. The system is imperfect, but the logic is sound: if something must recur, it should be tracked, and tracking should be triggered by time rather than by crisis. The personal version of this logic is to build a small "recurrence register" that captures the tasks that repeatedly ambush you, then ties them to your calendar or reminder system. The implication is that you are not trying to remember better. You are trying to remember less.

A second named, checkable example from intellectual history reinforces why naming recurrences matters. Linnaeus's system was powerful because it turned a world of endlessly repeated observation into a stable taxonomy. People could recognise a plant and place it. They did not have to start again each time. Your recurring tasks need a similar treatment. When a renewal arrives, it should be recognisable as "one of those". It should have a place to go. It should have a predictable handling routine. Otherwise it becomes an orphan each time, requiring you to recreate the context and to suffer the small shock of surprise.

The psychology of "ambush" is also worth understanding. A recurring task feels like an ambush when it arrives as a demand rather than as a prompt. Demands trigger threat response: urgency, irritation, avoidance. Prompts invite planning. A prompt says, "This is coming; you can choose when to address it." That choice changes the emotional tone. It also reduces the likelihood of avoidance, because avoidance thrives on amorphous timing. If something can be done "any time", it often becomes "no time". If something has a defined prompt, it becomes a bounded decision: handle now, schedule, delegate, or delete. Again, the same logic as triage returns. The system becomes consistent.

The key is to separate the recurring task itself from the work it requires when it appears. A renewal might require checking terms, making a call, comparing options, updating details, or simply confirming. The recurring element is the fact that it returns. The work element can vary. By capturing the recurrence, you prevent the task from living as a vague mental note. You move it into a time-based system where it can be revisited with the right level of attention. This is where "awareness not detailed budgeting" aligns with recurrence management. The aim is to avoid being surprised, not to optimise every choice.

A limitation must be faced, because not every recurring task deserves a place in your system. Over-registering can create noise. If you attempt to track every possible annual, quarterly, and monthly obligation, you will produce a reminder cascade that you begin to ignore. Ignored reminders are dangerous because they train you to distrust your own prompts. The reconciliation is to select what tends to ambush you with consequences: the renewals and recurring obligations that reliably create stress when handled late. The standard is pragmatic. A reminder should earn its place by preventing a scramble.

Another limitation is that not all recurring tasks are truly time-based. Some are event-based. A car service depends on mileage. A health check might depend on symptoms or life stage. A professional renewal might depend on changes in role. Even here, the principle holds: the reminder system does not need perfect precision. It needs to create a prompt at a plausible time to review whether action is needed. The prompt is not the action. It is the cue for a decision. Decisions are what reduce open loops.

The motif for this subchapter is the calendar tickler file, the old office practice of placing documents in dated folders so they resurface when needed. The modern equivalent can be digital, but the idea is the same. A tickler file prevents you from repeatedly remembering to remember. It externalises recurrence. Recurrence, once externalised, becomes less emotionally charged because it stops being a looming unknown. It becomes a scheduled review. Scheduled reviews are calmer than surprise demands.

Recurrence management also interacts with self-trust in a quiet way. People often carry recurring tasks mentally because they do not trust any system to remind them at the right time. They have been burned by missed reminders or by overly early prompts. They therefore keep a mental list: remember to renew, remember to book, remember to check. This list creates background stress, and ironically it increases the chance of forgetting because it competes with other mental demands. A well-placed reminder restores trust not by being clever but by being reliable: it appears when it can be acted on. When reliability is established, the mind stops patrolling.

The moment to collect recurring tasks is not the moment of ambush. It is the calm moment when you are already doing maintenance, like the Sunday reset. That is where the pattern is visible. That is where you can look back at what ambushed you last month or last season and decide to remove the surprise next time. Each new recurring task is then treated not as a fresh irritation but as a candidate for the tickler file. If it keeps returning, it earns a prompt.

The forward test is therefore simple and slightly uncomfortable. Which recurring obligation keeps arriving as a surprise even though you know it recurs, and what would change if you stopped relying on your head as the tickler file and gave that obligation a timed prompt that surfaces it before it becomes urgent?

Chapter 10
Relationship and wellbeing check-ins

A person notices, midweek, that they have been avoiding a conversation. Not dramatically. Just a slight detour each time the topic edges into view. They reply warmly to messages while leaving one thread untouched. They keep meaning to ask how someone is really doing, then run out of time and send a lighter text instead. They feel a small pinch of guilt about a friend they have not checked in on, a family situation they have half-acknowledged, a worry they keep circling without naming. Nothing is visibly on fire. And yet something is accumulating.

Another person believes they have no time for feelings. Their week is packed, their responsibilities real, their energy finite. They tell themselves they will deal with the emotional stuff when things calm down, as if calm were a season that arrives on a calendar. It does not. The emotional backlog grows quietly, like laundry piling behind a closed door: you can pretend it is not there, but the smell eventually changes the whole house. Then a small trigger arrives, and the reaction is out of proportion, not because the person is fragile, but because the backlog has been carrying weight for too long.

Neglect becomes noise.

That is the central tension of relationship and wellbeing check-ins. Emotional load behaves like life admin in one crucial way: what is unresolved keeps resurfacing. The mind replays conversations, rehearses what might be said, worries at the edges of uncertainty, and carries concerns as half-formed loops. This is not indulgence. It is cognition trying to find closure. When the Sunday reset ignores emotional backlog, the week may still be organised on paper and yet feel strangely heavy, because the heart is carrying open loops the calendar cannot see. The reset is not meant to turn life into a spreadsheet. It is meant to stop attention leaking. Emotional leakage counts.

The stakes here are both immediate and slow. Immediately, unresolved emotional load steals attention in the same scattered way unfinished tasks do: it interrupts focus, sharpens irritability, and makes rest less restful because the mind uses quiet moments to replay what it has not faced. Slowly, it shapes relationships by default. When connection relies on leftover time, it is often the first thing squeezed, which creates a delayed cost: distance, regret, and a sense of living alongside people rather than with them. A week can be efficient and still feel empty. That emptiness is not solved by better task management. It is solved by making space for human contact and emotional honesty in small, doable ways.

The trade-off is delicate. People fear that if they open the door to emotional backlog, the door will not close. They imagine a Sunday reset turning into a heavy therapy session or a long emotional inventory. That fear is one reason people keep emotional concerns vague. Vagueness feels safer. Yet vagueness is precisely what makes worries stick. When something is unnamed, it cannot be handled, only carried. The way through is not to dive into every feeling. It is to notice where emotional load is building and to choose one next step that creates a state change: a message sent, a time to talk set, a decision made about what you are willing to carry.

The motif for this chapter is the knot in the chest. It is not poetic. It is physical. Many people can tell when something is unresolved because the body registers it: a tightness when a name appears, a tired dread when a particular topic comes up, a subtle resistance to opening a chat thread, a sense of heaviness when thinking about a family need. The knot is information. It is the body's version of the mental ping. Ignoring it does not untie it. It simply leaves it there, pulling on the week.

Planned connection matters because relying on "spare time" is a structural mistake. Spare time is not a reliable resource. It is what is left after everything else has taken its share, and everything else tends to be loud. Relationships are often quiet until they are in pain. A planned call, a shared walk, a brief check-in at home, or a deliberate moment of attention does not need to be grand to be real. It needs to be chosen. Choice is what turns connection from an afterthought into a practice. When connection is planned, it reduces last-minute scrambling and the awkward feeling of having neglected people you care about until guilt forces a rushed gesture.

This chapter continues the book's insistence on sustainability and clean endings. Emotional check-ins must fit inside the Sunday reset rather than take it over. They must respect real constraints, including privacy, energy, and the complexity of relationships. The point is not to fix everything. It is to reduce emotional open loops by naming them and by making one concrete move that prevents the week from being governed by avoidance. Done well, this does not make life sentimental. It makes life more stable, because stability is not only about time and tasks; it is about the emotional weather you carry into each day.

The path here begins by noticing the emotional backlog without turning it into self-criticism or a personal trial. It then moves towards planned connection as a form of intentionality, so relationships do not depend on whatever fragments of attention remain after the urgent has taken everything. Both moves are small. Their effect is not small. They change what the week feels like from the inside.

The unresolved friction that pulls us into the work is quietly confronting. Which relationship or worry are you carrying as a background loop because you have not named it, and what would shift if you chose one next step that turns the knot into something scheduled, spoken, or at least acknowledged?

Noticing emotional backlog

In 1986 at Southern Methodist University in Dallas, psychologist James W. Pennebaker and Sandra Beall published a study in which people wrote about upsetting experiences, and the work became widely cited for a simple implication: unprocessed emotion does not vanish just because a person stays busy (Pennebaker and Beall, 1986). Whatever one makes of the later debates and replications, the original scene is easy to picture. A desk. A blank page. A mind that would rather not go near certain thoughts. The outcome was not moral improvement. It was a shift in what the mind had to carry.

That carrying is the ordinary problem. Emotional backlog is not melodrama. It is the accumulation of unresolved conversations, worries that loop without landing, and quiet family needs that are noticed but not named. It often begins with a small avoidance: a message not replied to because the reply requires honesty; a conversation postponed because it might be uncomfortable; a recurring worry kept vague because clarity would force a decision. The mind treats these items like open loops. They resurface. They tug at attention in the margins of other tasks. They produce a background hum that can make a well-organised week still feel heavy.

The knot returns.

The knot is not metaphorical for many people. It is a bodily cue: a tightness when a particular person's name appears, a faint dread when a topic comes up, a slight resistance to opening a chat thread, a tendency to change the subject in one's own mind. These cues are often dismissed as irrational, yet they are often accurate signals of unfinished emotional business. The mind avoids the issue because it anticipates complexity, conflict, or pain. Avoidance provides immediate relief. It also creates a recurring cost: each time the issue resurfaces, the mind pays attention again without gaining closure.

Emotional backlog behaves like the admin backlog described earlier in the book because both are forms of unresolved information. A bill left unopened is frightening because its contents are unknown. A conversation left unhad is frightening for the same reason: the outcome is unknown, and the stakes feel personal. Uncertainty invites monitoring. Monitoring is tiring. The mind keeps checking the emotional perimeter: what if they are upset, what if I am wrong, what if I cannot handle the response, what if this becomes bigger. None of these questions is answered by silence. Silence simply keeps the questions alive.

This is why "noticing" matters more than it sounds. Noticing is not wallowing. It is classification. It is the act of identifying which emotional items are repeatedly consuming attention and naming them as items rather than letting them remain part of the atmosphere. When something is part of the atmosphere, it cannot be addressed; it can only be endured. When it is an item, it can be given a next state. The key is that the next state does not have to be resolution. It can be a single stabilising move: a message that acknowledges, a date set for a talk, a clear boundary stated, a request for clarification, a decision to stop circling and seek support. The mental shift is from indefinite rumination to contained action.

A good way to understand the difference is to compare two internal experiences that look similar from the outside. In the first, a person is "thinking about it" all week: replaying what was said, imagining what might be said, drafting an apology or a defence in their head, anticipating the other person's reaction. The thinking is vivid and repetitive. It produces fatigue, not progress. In the second, the person notices the same concern and does something small but decisive that changes its status in the world: they send a short message that names the issue, or they schedule a time to talk, or they write down what they need in one sentence and put it somewhere they will revisit deliberately. The thinking may still be uncomfortable. It is also less sticky, because the mind can sense movement. This is the difference between rumination and processing. Rumination circles. Processing changes state.

This distinction has been studied across several strands of psychology, often with different language, but the underlying observation is consistent. Worry and rumination tend to be repetitive and abstract; they keep problems alive without resolving them. Emotional processing tends to be more concrete: it makes meaning, identifies specific concerns, and often leads to specific behavioural steps. Susan Nolen-Hoeksema's work on rumination, for example, helped clarify how repetitive, passive focus on distress can prolong low mood and interfere with problem-solving (Nolen-Hoeksema, 1991). The point here is not to diagnose anyone or to medicalise normal life. It is to name a pattern that time-conscious people recognise: the same worry can consume hours without producing the one sentence or one action that would begin to settle it.

A second checkable anchor shows how the power of naming and small state changes appears in relationship research without requiring romanticised notions of "perfect communication". John Gottman's research programme at the University of Washington, widely associated with observational studies of couples from the late twentieth century onwards, emphasised that patterns of interaction and repair matter: what people do when things go wrong, how they return to safety, how they respond to bids for connection (Gottman, 1994). The relevance here is not the lab apparatus or the headlines about prediction. It is a quieter point: relationships are maintained through small acts that keep disconnection from accumulating. Emotional backlog often forms when repair is postponed, when bids are missed, when minor ruptures are left to fossilise. Noticing is the step that prevents fossilisation. It makes repair possible because it reveals where repair is needed.

Noticing emotional backlog also involves distinguishing between different kinds of load. Some backlog is relational: something needs to be said to someone else. Some is intrapersonal: a worry about work, identity, competence, or meaning that keeps returning because it has not been translated into a question you can answer. Some is systemic: ongoing family needs, care responsibilities, or long-running pressures that cannot be "solved" but can be acknowledged and managed with more clarity. Each kind creates its own style of ping. Relational load often comes with an urge to avoid contact. Intrapersonal load often comes with late-night mental rehearsals and sudden pangs during quiet moments. Systemic load often comes with a low, steady fatigue and resentment at the amount that must be held.

The important move is to stop treating all emotional discomfort as a single category. Some discomfort is a signal that something needs attention. Some discomfort is the normal friction of being human in a complex life. Noticing is about telling the difference. When the mind keeps circling the same worry, it is often because the worry has not been reduced to a clear proposition. "I am worried about work" is too vague to resolve. "I am worried that I will miss a deadline" can be checked against the calendar. "I am worried that I have let someone down" can be tested by contacting them. "I am worried that this situation will not change" might require a longer conversation, a boundary, or an acceptance that you cannot control everything. In each case, the worry becomes more tractable when it is named precisely.

Precision does not make emotion disappear. It makes emotion workable.

This is why the "one next step" matters. Emotional backlog tends to feel infinite because it is rarely one task. It is a tangle of feelings, assumptions, memories, and future fears. Attempting to resolve the whole tangle in one sitting is unrealistic and often counterproductive. The next step is not meant to solve the entire issue. It is meant to reduce the cognitive load by creating a small commitment that the mind can trust. A scheduled conversation is a commitment. A message that names what has been avoided is a commitment. A written sentence that clarifies what you are actually worried about is a commitment. Commitments reduce monitoring because they give the mind a timeline. Without a timeline, the mind keeps pinging to prevent forgetting. With a timeline, the mind can stand down a little.

The knot motif helps here because knots tighten when pulled at the wrong angle. Many people pull at emotional knots through internal argument: rehearsing, imagining, second-guessing. The knot does not loosen. It tightens. A better angle is often externalisation: naming the issue in plain language, even if only to yourself, and choosing the smallest action that changes its state. This is not a promise of emotional comfort. It is a shift from helplessness to agency. Agency, even modest agency, reduces dread.

A credible limitation needs to be stated to keep this honest. Not all emotional backlog should be handled through direct conversation or quick steps. Some situations are unsafe. Some relationships are abusive or coercive, and "naming the issue" can increase risk. Some worries are signs of deeper distress that may require professional support. Some family needs are chronic and cannot be resolved by a message. In these cases, the principle remains but the application changes. The aim is still to reduce uncontained monitoring and repeated rumination. The "next step" might be to seek appropriate support, to set a boundary, to document what is happening, or to create a safer plan rather than to confront. Educationally, the key point is that noticing backlog does not obligate anyone to act in a way that increases harm. It obligates clarity: what is being carried, why, and what form of response is actually appropriate.

Another limitation is more subtle: some people can turn noticing into self-surveillance. They start scanning their feelings obsessively, treating every discomfort as a problem to solve. That approach can create a new kind of noise. Emotional life is not a set of admin tickets. The reconciliation is to keep the Sunday reset's broader discipline in view: containment and sustainability. Noticing is a brief check-in, not a deep dive. Its job is to identify the items that are repeatedly consuming attention, not to analyse every mood. The metric is whether attention becomes freer after the check-in. If the check-in creates more rumination, it has become the wrong kind of attention.

Noticing emotional backlog also improves planning in a way that is rarely discussed openly. When a person has a heavy unresolved conversation hanging over them, their capacity for deep work often shrinks. They may still sit at the desk and try, but attention will drift back to the unresolved. When a person is worrying about a family need, they may struggle to concentrate even if the calendar looks open. Energy is not only physical; it is emotional. This is why the Sunday reset includes relationships and wellbeing. A plan that ignores emotional load is often a plan that fails, then blames the person for "lacking focus". Noticing is a correction. It brings the hidden constraints into view.

The practical question at the heart of this is therefore not sentimental. It is diagnostic. Emotional backlog is not defined by big feelings. It is defined by repeated returns of the same thought, the same avoidance, the same knot. When you notice those returns, you can treat them as signals rather than as failures. You can ask what the signal is pointing to: a conversation that needs scheduling, a boundary that needs stating, a worry that needs specificity, a family need that requires coordination, or a grief that needs acknowledgement rather than suppression.

The knot returns one last time, because it is the simplest test. When you think about the week ahead, where does your body tighten slightly, and what, exactly, is that tension asking you to name?

Planning connection on purpose

In Cambridge, Massachusetts, in 1973, the psychiatrist Robert N. Butler introduced the term "life review" to describe a common process in later life: people naturally look back and weigh what mattered, what was repaired, what was left undone (Butler, 1963; Butler, 1973). The idea has since taken on many interpretations, but its simplest implication is quietly instructive for anyone planning a week. When people regret, they rarely regret that the inbox was not cleared. They regret that connection was postponed until "later" and later never arrived.

Later is a hungry word.

It eats the spare moments that relationships are supposed to live on. Many people treat connection as something that will happen in the margins: a call when the week calms down, a visit when work is lighter, a proper conversation when everyone is less tired. The intention is sincere. The structure is flawed. The margins are where everything else goes to hide, and relationships lose to whatever is loudest or most urgent. This is how good intentions turn into a quiet thinning: not a dramatic rupture, but a slow drift where people still care yet stop showing it in ways that feel nourishing.

Planning connection on purpose is a structural correction. It treats relationships the way this book treats everything else that matters: as commitments that deserve a home, not as hopes that deserve a shrug. The goal is not to schedule intimacy like a corporate meeting. The goal is to remove reliance on leftover time. Leftover time is unreliable. When connection relies on it, connection becomes intermittent, and intermittent connection creates a particular kind of background stress: the nagging sense of being behind on one's own relationships.

A small scene reveals how this happens. A person thinks warmly of a friend and mentally composes a message while walking to work. They do not send it because they are busy and because it feels slightly inadequate: they want to say something real, not a perfunctory "how are you". The message remains unsent. The thought resurfaces a few days later, now carrying guilt. The person avoids it again because guilt makes the reach-out feel even harder. A week passes. Nothing terrible occurs. Something still changes: the relationship is left to chance rather than tended by intention. The concept here is drift under good intentions. The implication is that planned connection is not primarily about time. It is about lowering the activation energy required to show up.

The best argument for planning connection is not sentimental. It is behavioural. When connection is not planned, it tends to happen in two unhelpful forms: rushed and reactive. Rushed connection is the hurried call squeezed between tasks, where attention is partial and the conversation ends abruptly. Reactive connection is the crisis check-in, prompted by guilt, bad news, or a sudden realisation that too long has passed. Both forms can be necessary sometimes. Neither forms a stable relational rhythm. A planned moment, even a small one, changes the quality of attention available. It creates a container where you do not have to multitask your way through care.

Research on relationships often highlights the importance of small, repeated behaviours rather than grand gestures. John Gottman's work, for example, emphasised "bids" for connection and the pattern of turning towards rather than away in everyday moments (Gottman, 1994). The language may sound clinical, but the lived experience is simple. People reach out in small ways. They notice. They respond. When those small behaviours are squeezed out by busyness, relationships do not usually explode. They thin. Planning connection on purpose is a way of protecting those small behaviours from the tyranny of the urgent, by giving them a time and a place to occur.

Planning also reduces social risk, which is a surprising barrier for many competent adults. People hesitate to reach out because they worry about bothering someone, interrupting them, or revealing need. When connection is spontaneous, it requires a moment of courage: "Will this be welcomed?" When connection is planned with mutual agreement, that courage is required less often. The plan converts an uncertain social move into a shared expectation. Expectation is calming. It reduces the fear of being inconvenient. It also reduces the tendency to postpone because the moment is vague. Vague moments become never. Planned moments become real.

The motif for this subchapter is the table. Not a grand table, just a small one. The table is where people sit down long enough to be present. Many households and friendships have lost the table metaphorically, not because they do not care, but because life has turned into a sequence of standing conversations, scrolling companionship, and half-attention. Planning connection is a way of putting the table back into the week, even briefly. A midweek call is a table. A shared walk is a table in motion. A short check-in at home is a table if the phone is down and attention is up. The table motif matters because it highlights the goal: not mere contact, but presence.

Connection also benefits the rest of the Sunday reset in a practical way. Relationships generate obligations and emotional loops when neglected: misunderstandings that grow, worries that circle, resentments that become heavier with silence. Planned connection prevents some of these loops from forming, which reduces the emotional backlog described in the previous subchapter. It also creates a more realistic week. If you know you will speak to a parent midweek, you can stop carrying the concern as a constant background thought. If you know you will have a short check-in with a partner about logistics, you can stop doing mental rehearsal alone. In this sense, planned connection is not a competing commitment. It is a way of preventing other commitments from becoming chaotic because the relational base is unstable.

There is a credible limitation worth acknowledging. Some relationships cannot be "scheduled" in a straightforward way. People have conflicting schedules. Some relationships are strained. Some people do not welcome planned contact and prefer spontaneity. Others are dealing with grief, illness, or complex dynamics where a simple weekly rhythm is not possible. Planning connection is not a universal fix. The reconciliation is to keep the principle while adapting the form. The principle is intentionality: do not rely entirely on leftover time and accidental windows. Even in complex dynamics, intentionality can mean agreeing a time to talk, sending a message that names your availability, choosing a regular small gesture that signals care without demanding a heavy conversation. The plan should fit the relationship, not force it into a template.

Another limitation is that planning can be used as a substitute for actual presence. A person can schedule calls and still show up distracted, treating the calendar entry as proof of care while the mind is elsewhere. This is a real risk for highly driven people who treat everything as a task. The reconciliation is to treat planned connection as a commitment to attention, not merely to time. The point is to create a container where attention can be less fragmented. If the planned moment becomes another multitasked slot, it loses its value and can even breed resentment. Planning is the doorway. Presence is the room.

Planned connection also interacts with wellbeing in a non-sentimental way. Humans regulate stress through contact. Even brief supportive interactions can change the feel of a week, not because they solve problems, but because they remind you that you are not carrying everything alone. This is not a claim that connection replaces professional support when needed or that relationships should be used as therapy. It is a recognition that isolation magnifies stress and that intentional connection can reduce the sense of being under constant pressure. A week with small planned moments of contact often feels less brittle, because there are points of warmth and reality-check built in.

The table motif returns at the end because it points to the forward test. Many people say they do not have time for relationships, but what they often mean is that they do not have unclaimed time. Planning connection does not create more hours. It changes what the existing hours are used for. The question is therefore sharp and practical. If connection continues to rely on leftover time, who in your life will quietly receive the leftovers, and what would change if one small table in the week were placed deliberately, before the urgent takes everything?

Chapter 11
Declutter loops for physical and digital mess

A person comes home, drops their keys on the nearest flat surface, and tells themselves they will put everything away later. Later does not arrive. The surface becomes a landing strip: post, receipts, a spare charger, a half-used notebook, a bag that should be hung up, a parcel that needs returning. By the end of the week, the landing strip has become a pile, and the pile has become a project. The person does not feel messy. They feel vaguely harried, because every time they pass the pile it asks a question: what is this, where does it go, is it important, will I regret ignoring it. The home begins to whisper.

Meanwhile, the phone vibrates with small, bright demands. An app update. A promotional email. A notification that looks urgent until it is opened and reveals itself as noise. Photos accumulate. Downloads multiply. Screenshots become a second inbox. Each item is tiny. Together they create a fog of attention. The person finds themselves checking compulsively, not because they are addicted to technology in some moral sense, but because the system is constantly producing signals and the brain is not good at ignoring signals that might matter. Physical clutter and digital clutter begin to feel like one problem: too many unresolved decisions living in too many places.

Clutter is delayed decision-making.

That is the central tension of this chapter. Many people imagine clutter as an aesthetic issue, a matter of taste or discipline. In reality, clutter is often a loop that has been left open. Each object on a surface is an unanswered question. Each unread email is an unmade decision. Each download kept "just in case" is a refusal to choose what matters. The cost is not only the physical inconvenience of mess or the digital inconvenience of storage. The cost is attention leakage. The mind keeps noticing the unresolved, keeps pinging, keeps rechecking, and in that constant noticing it loses the ease that makes life feel manageable.

The stakes are immediate because clutter produces friction in the moments when you can least afford it. You cannot find your keys. You misplace a document. You miss a message because it is buried under irrelevant ones. You lose time searching, and the search turns into irritation, which turns into sharper speech and a more frantic day. Friction is how small messes become relational and emotional problems, not because people are petty, but because time pressure and repeated inconvenience lower patience. A functional environment protects attention and mood. A dysfunctional one taxes both.

The deeper stakes are about the kind of life you are rehearsing. When you allow piles and notifications to build unchecked, you teach your brain that nothing ever really ends. There is always more to handle, more to read, more to sort, more to decide. That "always more" feeling is exhausting because it removes the possibility of clean endings. Clean endings are what make the Sunday reset sustainable. Without them, even rest feels provisional, because the mind suspects it will have to keep remembering what the environment refuses to resolve.

This chapter continues the book's focus on control without perfection. Decluttering here is not an attempt to curate a minimalist identity or create a show-home aesthetic. The aim is function: key surfaces that remain usable, an inbox that signals rather than shouts, a device that is not a junk drawer, a simple exit route for items that should leave the home. These are not grand goals. They are small structural choices that prevent the same mess from becoming the same project every month. The week does not need a dramatic purge. It needs a reliable loop.

The motif for this chapter is the junk drawer, both literal and digital. A junk drawer is comforting in the short term because it postpones decisions. It is also costly because it forces decisions later under worse conditions, usually when you are looking for something quickly and the drawer offers chaos instead. Phones and laptops become junk drawers in the same way: downloads, duplicates, forgotten screenshots, and a backlog of notifications that create the sensation of being perpetually behind. A reset loop does not eliminate the existence of small mess. It prevents the junk drawer from becoming the governing model of your environment.

The path here starts with the physical friction points that create daily drag, using a quick loop that keeps surfaces functional rather than letting piles mature into projects. It then moves into digital noise, where notifications mimic urgency and pull attention away from what matters, and into the quieter mess of photos and downloads that turn devices into storage units rather than tools. It ends with a simple, ongoing route for items leaving the home, because decluttering only becomes sustainable when exit is easy. The emphasis throughout is continuity: small loops repeated regularly rather than dramatic efforts repeated rarely.

The unresolved friction that pulls us into the practical work is simple enough to be felt. Which clutter in your life is not really about stuff at all, but about a decision you keep postponing, and what would change if you built a small loop that ends those decisions before they turn into noise?

Resetting your key surfaces

In Frankfurt am Main in 1926, the architect Margarete Schuette-Lihotzky designed the Frankfurt Kitchen as a compact workspace intended to reduce wasted movement and make daily domestic work less exhausting (Schuette-Lihotzky, 1926). The point was not decoration. It was function. It treated the home as a system where small, repeated motions either flow smoothly or snag, and where snagging, repeated daily, becomes a kind of chronic stress. The kitchen was an argument that the smallest design choices can change the whole rhythm of a week.

A key surface is a design choice you make every day, whether you mean to or not. You place your keys somewhere. You put post down somewhere. You drop a bag, a charger, a coat, a receipt, a cup, a note. The place you put it becomes the place it lives. Then the surface becomes a message about what your week is doing: either you are returning things to their homes, or you are creating new homes out of whatever is nearest. Most clutter is not hoarding. It is the creation of accidental homes.

Surfaces are decision machines.

The most useful way to think about key surfaces is not as "messy areas" but as workstations. The entryway is where departures and arrivals happen. The kitchen counter is where meals and small logistics are assembled. The bedside is where the day ends and begins. These surfaces are touched daily. That is why they matter. They are the points where friction is most likely to be felt and least likely to be explicitly planned for. When they are clogged, the home stops supporting the week and starts interrupting it. When they are clear enough, the week runs with less needless interruption.

The central claim is plain: resetting key surfaces reduces attention leakage by reducing repeated micro-decisions. A cluttered surface forces decisions at the wrong time. "Where do I put this?" "Is this important?" "Should I keep this?" "Why is this here?" These questions appear when you are tired, rushing, or already overloaded. When you answer them under pressure, you make worse decisions or postpone decisions, and postponed decisions become piles. Piles are not neutral. They produce a low-grade cognitive load because they are visible, ambiguous, and unresolved. The mind keeps noticing them. Noticing is not a moral judgement. It is a demand for closure.

A scene makes the mechanism almost embarrassing. A person comes in, drops keys on the counter, drops post beside the keys, places a bag on a chair, leaves shoes by the door. None of this feels consequential. It is efficient in the moment. The next morning, the person looks for the keys, which are under yesterday's post. The post includes something important, but the person does not have time to read it. The bag is still on the chair, in the way, so they move it to the floor. Now there are two places bags can live. The surface now contains more objects. Each object is a delayed decision. The home begins to behave like an inbox with no triage: items arrive, are placed somewhere, and then sit in an unresolved state. The implication is that surface clutter is not about being untidy; it is about leaving decisions in physical form.

This is why the "return, bin, relocate" loop is powerful. It is not a grand decluttering programme. It is a small repeated logic that converts physical ambiguity into clear fates. Return means an item already has a home and should go back there. Bin means the item is rubbish, a packaging remnant, a receipt that does not matter, a piece of paper with no continuing value, something that will only become a future decision if you keep it. Relocate means the item does not belong on this surface and does not yet have a clear home here, so it must be moved to the place where a decision can be made or where it belongs. The loop is blunt because bluntness reduces hesitation. Hesitation is where piles are born.

The loop works because it respects a principle that shows up in the earlier chapters: decisions create closure, and closure reduces monitoring. An item returned is closed. An item binned is closed. An item relocated is not necessarily closed, but it is contained, and containment prevents the surface from becoming a storage unit for unresolved life. In other words, the loop is a physical version of triage. It does not attempt to solve every problem. It prevents surfaces from becoming projects.

A second checkable anchor reinforces why this kind of small repeated loop matters. Christine Frederick's *Household Engineering: Scientific Management in the Home*, published in New York in 1919, applied time-and-motion thinking to domestic life, with the basic idea that repetitive tasks become less draining when their steps are simplified and their environments support them (Frederick, 1919). The framing belongs to its era, but the insight transfers. Household friction is often the result of repeated unnecessary motions and repeated unnecessary decisions. Key surfaces are where those decisions concentrate, because they are the most convenient dumping grounds. A reset loop reduces that concentration.

The key surfaces named here are not arbitrary. They are where time pressure and attention pressure intersect. The entryway is where leaving the house turns into a scramble when essentials are missing or scattered. The kitchen counter is where evening fatigue meets the need for food and logistics, a moment when decision quality tends to be low. The bedside is where late-night mental chatter meets the desire for rest, and where physical clutter can translate directly into psychological clutter because the first and last things you see frame your day. A bed-side pile is not just objects. It is a set of unresolved questions delivered to your nervous system at the exact moments it is trying to settle.

The practical effect of resetting these surfaces is not aesthetic satisfaction, though that may occur. It is a reduction in search time and irritation. Search time is a visible metric: how often you look for keys, glasses, documents, chargers. Irritation is also measurable in behaviour: the sharp tone when someone asks where something is, the habitual blaming, the rushed movements, the feeling that the house is working against you.

A surface reset does not fix deeper life problems. It removes a recurring, avoidable source of friction that steals attention daily.

There is a limitation worth stating to keep this honest. Some homes are small, shared, and short on storage. Surfaces become cluttered partly because there is nowhere else for things to go. In such environments, "return" may not be possible because there is no true home for certain items, and "relocate" may simply move the pile from one surface to another. The reconciliation is to narrow the definition of key surfaces even further: protect one small section of a counter, one spot by the door, one clear bedside area. Function does not require spaciousness. It requires a protected zone where the loop can operate. Even a small clear patch can reduce daily micro-stress if it holds the essentials.

Another limitation is social. In shared households, one person can reset surfaces and another can immediately refill them. This can create resentment and make the practice feel pointless. The loop still has value, but its aim shifts. It becomes less about permanent order and more about making the environment workable repeatedly, and about creating shared defaults where possible: a consistent place for keys, a consistent place for post to be processed, a consistent bin for outgoing items. Defaults reduce conflict because they reduce the need for negotiation at the moment of use. Negotiation is expensive when everyone is tired.

The motif that unifies this subchapter is the landing strip. Key surfaces are landing strips for objects and decisions. When the strip is clear enough, arrivals and departures are smoother. When it is cluttered, every landing becomes a collision. The "return, bin, relocate" loop is simply the habit of keeping the strip usable, so that the week can move without catching on the same debris day after day.

The forward test is therefore not about tidiness. It is about function under pressure. Which surface in your home routinely becomes a decision pile, and what would change if you ran a brief loop that forced every item on it into one of three fates before the pile has time to mature into a project?

Email and notification triage

On 1 April 2004, Google launched Gmail from Mountain View, California, and email quietly changed shape for millions of people: the inbox became something you could search and archive rather than something you had to file perfectly to survive (Google, 2004). The innovation was not only technical. It was behavioural. It suggested that a large flow of incoming messages could be tolerated if retrieval was reliable and if attention was not forced to treat every new arrival as an emergency. The idea was liberating. The lived reality for many people, however, has been less liberation than saturation.

Those red badges never sleep.

A modern inbox and a modern phone are not just communication tools. They are signal machines. They produce constant prompts, some meaningful, many irrelevant, most mixed. A notification arrives and it does not merely deliver information; it changes posture. The mind turns towards it, even if only for a moment, because it might matter. That "might" is the key. Uncertainty makes signals powerful. An unread message could contain a deadline, a request, or a minor newsletter. The brain cannot tell from the outside, so it checks. Checking becomes a habit. Habits become a baseline. Before long, the day is punctuated by attention shifts so frequent they feel like normal life.

The central problem is that alerts mimic urgency. They borrow the emotional tone of emergencies without the factual basis. A bell, a vibration, a red badge, a subject line in capitals: these cues are designed to be hard to ignore. They are not malicious in the abstract; they are efficient at getting attention. Yet attention is not an infinite resource. When attention is repeatedly captured by low-value signals, deep work, meaningful conversations, and even rest become porous. The Sunday reset exists to reduce attention leakage. Digital noise is one of the most common leak points because it creates open loops by the dozen.

A small scene shows how quickly this happens. Someone is writing, analysing, or preparing, and a notification appears: a new email, a chat message, a calendar reminder, an app prompt. They glance. The content is minor, but now the mind has been pulled into a different context. A second message arrives. They respond quickly "just to clear it". Another message appears that is more complex, so they mark it unread to return later. Now there is a new open loop. They attempt to return to the original task, but the mind retains a residue of the interruption: the unfinished reply, the awareness of other messages waiting, the itch to check again. The concept is attention residue, the phenomenon where a portion of attention remains stuck on the previous task after switching. Sophie Leroy's research described how switching leaves a residue that can impair performance on the next task (Leroy, 2009). The implication is not that checking an email is immoral. It is that frequent checking is expensive, and the cost is paid in fragmented thinking.

The cost is amplified by the way notification systems blur the boundary between signal and noise. A message from a colleague and a promotional offer can arrive with the same visual priority. An urgent request and a routine update can share a red badge. The system does not know what matters to you; it knows what was sent. The mind responds by treating a large proportion of incoming items as potentially important, because missing a truly important item has consequences. This is why people check reflexively. The reflex is not weakness. It is risk management in an environment that refuses to label risk accurately.

Email triage is therefore not about "inbox zero" as a lifestyle. It is about regaining control of what deserves your attention. The simplest triage categories are behavioural rather than philosophical: act on what genuinely needs a response and can be handled quickly; defer what requires more time or information by giving it a stable next step; delegate what belongs with someone else; delete what is irrelevant, promotional, or no longer meaningful. The categories matter less than the principle: every incoming item must eventually have a fate, or it will continue to demand attention through monitoring. Monitoring is what makes inboxes feel heavy even when nothing terrible is inside.

Notification triage extends the same logic to the phone and the operating system. Alerts are not neutral. They are bids for attention. Some bids are valid. Many are opportunistic. If every app is allowed to ring the bell, the bell becomes meaningless, and yet it continues to pull attention because it is loud and uncertain. The result is a peculiar fatigue: not the fatigue of doing too much work, but the fatigue of being interrupted. Task switching research has long suggested that switching imposes performance costs, even when people believe they are multitasking effectively (Rubinstein, Meyer, and Evans, 2001). When alerts drive switching, the environment is effectively imposing an extra cognitive workload throughout the day.

A second checkable anchor makes this cultural shift easier to see. On 9 January 2007, Apple introduced the iPhone in San Francisco, an event that helped accelerate a transition from occasional digital checking to continuous digital availability (Apple, 2007). Again, the point is not nostalgia. It is structure. When a device is always with you, and when it is designed to display incoming signals instantly, the default becomes responsiveness. Responsiveness looks like competence. It can also become a trap. When the default is to respond to whatever appears, the week becomes shaped by interrupts rather than by intention. A Sunday reset that ignores notification hygiene is like mopping a floor while a tap is still running.

The objective here is reliability over features, and that includes the reliability of your own attention. A clean triage practice makes it easier to notice what genuinely requires your mind. It also reduces the creation of false urgency. Many people live with an internal sense that they are behind because they constantly see evidence of unfinished communication: unread counts, flagged messages, notification badges, pinned chats. These cues keep the mind in a state of unfinishedness. You can observe the effect in behaviour: repeated quick checks that produce no meaningful action, the habitual opening and closing of the inbox, the sense of needing to "just catch up" before starting important work. Triage reduces these behaviours by narrowing what is allowed to demand attention and by converting the rest into contained states.

The quiet motif for this subchapter is the bell. The bell is supposed to ring when something important happens. When it rings constantly, it stops being informative and becomes noise. Yet the body still reacts, because the bell has been trained into the nervous system. The work of triage is, in part, to retrain the bell: to reduce the number of times it rings, and to improve the correspondence between ringing and genuine importance. This is why unsubscribing and muting matter. They are not aesthetic preferences. They are signal-to-noise interventions. They reduce the number of low-value items that masquerade as urgent simply because they appear.

A third named example shows why design choices about noise matter at scale. When the UK Government Digital Service launched GOV.UK in October 2012, part of its aim was to reduce confusion by consolidating services and making pathways clearer rather than scattering information across multiple sites. The value was not merely convenience; it was reduced cognitive burden. Too many routes and too many competing signals increase error and frustration. Your inbox and your phone are personal versions of this problem. When there are too many channels and too many alerts, you create duplicate work, missed commitments, and the constant feeling of searching for the "real" message among the noise. Consolidation and triage reduce that burden by limiting where signals can appear and by giving each signal a clear fate.

There is a deeper psychological reason people resist unsubscribing and muting: they fear missing out on something important, or they fear that silence is irresponsible. That fear is rational in a noisy environment, because the environment has trained you that important things can arrive at any time and in any form. The solution is not to become indifferent. It is to create rules that protect you from randomness. Rules can be humble. "Only certain categories of people can ring through." "Only calendar reminders and direct messages notify." "Promotions do not get to interrupt." The function of a rule is not purity. It is predictability. Predictability reduces monitoring. Monitoring is the silent cost many people pay all day.

It is also worth acknowledging that constant alerts can become a substitute for feeling in control. Some people check because checking provides a micro-dose of certainty: nothing urgent has arrived, or something has arrived and can be handled. That certainty is briefly soothing. It is also a trap, because it trains the mind to seek certainty through frequent checking rather than through a reliable system of review. The Sunday reset is a reliable review. Daily life becomes calmer when the mind trusts that there are designated moments to handle communication, rather than relying on continuous scanning. Continuous scanning is not vigilance. It is erosion.

A credible limitation should be stated plainly. Some roles require real-time responsiveness: emergency services, on-call technical work, caregiving situations, time-sensitive logistics. For these roles, muting everything is neither realistic nor responsible. The reconciliation is to distinguish between necessary signals and elective noise. Even in high-responsiveness roles, not every signal is essential. The goal becomes reducing false positives: preventing non-critical alerts from masquerading as urgent, so that when something truly important arrives, it is not drowned in background ringing. A bell that rings for everything is dangerous in high-stakes contexts, because it trains people to ignore the bell. A bell that rings only for what matters is safer. The principle holds; the threshold changes.

Another limitation is that triage can become a performance. People can spend long sessions "organising email" by creating elaborate folders, rules, and labels that feel sophisticated but require constant maintenance. The system becomes the work. This mirrors the earlier trap of rewriting task lists instead of acting. A triage approach that holds up is minimal: enough structure to reduce searching and missed commitments, not so much that managing the structure becomes a second job. Reliability is again the measure. If you can capture and retrieve what matters and ignore what does not, the system is doing its job.

Notice also that triage is not only about the inbox. It is about your relationship with interruption. Interruptions are not merely inconvenient; they change how you think. Deep work depends on sustained attention. Relationships depend on presence. Rest depends on a nervous system that is not constantly bracing for the next ping. A lighter inbox supports a lighter mind not because fewer emails exist in the universe, but because fewer emails are allowed to live as unresolved loops. When a message is deleted, it closes. When it is deferred with a clear next step, it contains. When it is delegated cleanly, it transfers. When it is acted on, it finishes. Finishing is what quietens the ping.

The bell motif returns in the most practical way. If your phone and inbox ring constantly, you will either become jumpy or numb. Neither state supports a good week. A calmer system is one where the bell is meaningful. Meaningful bells allow you to ignore silence without guilt, because silence no longer feels like negligence. It feels like space you have deliberately protected.

The forward test is therefore not whether you can tolerate noise. Most people can, until they cannot. The question is whether the bell is telling the truth in your life: when your phone lights up, is it more often a genuine need or a manufactured interruption, and what would your week feel like if only the genuine needs were allowed to ring?

Managing photos and downloads

On 9 January 2007 in San Francisco, Apple introduced the iPhone and helped accelerate a shift in how ordinary people store their lives: not in albums on shelves, but in pockets, endlessly, as images and files that can be created with a tap (Apple, 2007). The change was not merely technological. It was psychological. When storage feels infinite and capture is effortless, the cost moves from creating to *curating*. The phone becomes a camera, a scanner, a notebook, and a filing cabinet. The laptop becomes a dumping ground for documents, screenshots, PDFs, drafts, and "things to look at later". Later arrives with a tired sigh.

Digital drawers fill silently.

And when they fill, the consequence is not only storage warnings or slow search. The deeper cost is attention leakage. A cluttered camera roll is not just messy; it is an archive of unmade decisions. A downloads folder packed with half-recognised files is not just untidy; it is a queue that was never acknowledged as a queue. Each screenshot saved "just in case" is a small bet against forgetting. Each duplicate photo is a tiny tax on future retrieval. Each file saved without a name is a promise that you will remember what it is. You will not. The mind, sensing this, compensates by checking more, re-downloading, re-screenshotting, and storing redundant copies. The system becomes unreliable, and unreliability makes you vigilant.

The central claim is that digital clutter is delayed triage. It is the same pattern as physical piles and inbox overload, translated into pixels. People capture with speed and postpone judgement. Postponing judgement is not always wrong; it is often sensible in the moment. The problem is when postponement has no return path. Without a minimal routine, digital capture becomes hoarding by default. The phone becomes a junk drawer. The laptop becomes a second junk drawer. Junk drawers are comforting in the short term because they postpone decisions. They are costly in the long term because they force decisions later under pressure, usually when you are trying to find something quickly and your attention is already stretched.

A small scene shows how "just in case" becomes a lifestyle. Someone receives an address in a message and screenshots it, meaning to add it to their calendar later. They also screenshot a booking confirmation, a parking sign, a list of items to buy, a reference number, a recipe, a note from school. Each screenshot is a sensible move in isolation. Over weeks, the camera roll becomes a second inbox with no subject lines and no triage. When the person needs the address, they scroll through hundreds of images, some meaningful, many trivial, all visually similar. The mind flinches. It cannot see the path. The concept here is retrieval friction. The implication is simple: the harder it is to retrieve, the more you will duplicate capture, and the more you duplicate capture, the harder retrieval becomes.

The same dynamic plays out on laptops. Downloads folders become a holding pen for PDFs, forms, and documents. Many are never used again, but their presence creates ambiguity. Is that the right version. Did I already submit this. Which file contains the key detail. Ambiguity invites monitoring. Monitoring shows up as repeated searching, re-opening, and that familiar itch to keep tabs open "so I do not forget". Research on task switching and attention suggests that switching between tasks carries cognitive costs (Rubinstein, Meyer, and Evans, 2001). Digital clutter increases switching because it forces repeated orientation. Each time you look for a file, you must interpret a messy set of options. Interpretation is a cognitive task. It steals attention from whatever you meant to do.

The solution is not to become a meticulous archivist. The solution is a micro-habit that keeps the drawers from becoming unopenable. The key is minimalism with intent: delete duplicates, file essentials, stop saving "just in case" items that do not serve a real future purpose. Deleting is not recklessness. It is a decision. Filing is not perfectionism. It is retrieval protection. "Stop saving just in case" is not a moral command. It is a recognition that your future self will pay for your current indecision. The aim is not to have a pristine device. The aim is to have a device that supports the week rather than interrupting it.

A named, checkable example helps make the "archive versus search" distinction tangible. Gmail's launch in April 2004 popularised the idea that one could keep a large volume of information and retrieve it via search, reducing the need for obsessive manual filing (Google, 2004). Many people took the lesson too far: they began to treat every digital space as an archive where everything can be found later. Yet search only works when items are in a system that is at least moderately coherent. A camera roll is not an indexed archive. A downloads folder filled with cryptically named files is not a searchable database in any meaningful sense. The implication is that "I will search later" is not a strategy unless the system supports searching. Otherwise it is simply deferral.

This is where the quiet motif of the junk drawer is useful again. A physical junk drawer often contains a few genuinely useful items and many things that are there because deciding their fate was inconvenient. Digital junk drawers are the same, except they multiply faster. People fear deleting because deletion feels irreversible. They fear filing because filing feels like work. So they postpone. The drawer grows. Growth increases dread, which increases avoidance, which increases growth. The loop tightens. A micro-habit breaks the loop by making the drawer small enough that it does not become emotionally charged.

There is also an emotional layer worth naming, especially for thoughtful professionals and students. Photos and downloads are not always "junk". They are often traces of identity and aspiration: articles to read, research papers to digest, course materials, ideas to explore, moments captured with people you love. The fear of deleting can therefore be a fear of losing possibility. This is why "just in case" is seductive. It protects the fantasy that you will return to all of it. The reality is that an overfull archive makes returning less likely because it is overwhelming. The implication is paradoxical: deleting can protect meaning by reducing noise. When the camera roll is smaller, the photos you keep are easier to find and revisit. When the downloads folder is lean, the documents that matter are easier to locate when needed.

A second checkable anchor helps because it frames digital clutter as a known cognitive phenomenon rather than a personal failing. Researchers have discussed "cognitive offloading", the practice of using external tools and environments to store information so the mind does not have to (Risko and Gilbert, 2016). Screenshots and downloads are forms of offloading. Offloading is useful when the external store is reliable. Offloading becomes harmful when the store is chaotic, because chaos forces the mind to keep a duplicate copy anyway. The person continues to rehearse "where it is" or "what it was called" because they do not trust retrieval. The goal of managing photos and downloads is to make offloading genuinely relieving by restoring some reliability to the store.

A credible limitation should be faced. Some people have legal, professional, or academic reasons to retain documents, receipts, and records. Others need to keep evidence for disputes or compliance. In such cases, deletion cannot be cavalier. The reconciliation is not to ignore the need for retention. It is to distinguish between what must be retained and what is merely "might be useful". Retention has criteria. "Might be useful" often does not. When retention is necessary, filing becomes even more important, because the cost of losing an essential document is higher. This is not advice about any specific legal or financial matter. It is a structural observation: if you must keep things, keep them in a form you can retrieve.

Another limitation is that some devices and apps already create automatic organisation: photo grouping, document scanning, cloud backups. These features can help. They can also create complacency. Automatic grouping does not solve the "just in case" habit, and it does not prevent the accumulation of near-duplicates, screenshots of transient information, or downloads saved without context. The micro-habit remains useful precisely because automation handles storage, not meaning. Meaning is your job. Meaning is deciding what matters.

The most powerful shift in this subchapter is to treat photos and downloads as *incoming* rather than as "stuff". Incoming requires triage. This aligns with the rest of the book. We do not leave open loops in our mind because we intend to suffer; we leave them because we have not assigned them fates. Digital items need fates too. Some should be deleted. Some should be filed. Some should be converted into a task or a calendar entry and then deleted. Some should be kept because they are genuinely valuable. The micro-habit is simply the repeated act of assigning fates before accumulation creates dread.

The junk drawer motif returns at the point where people often stall: the fear of regret. What if I delete something I later need. What if I file it wrong. What if I cannot find it again. These fears are reasonable in an unreliable system. The goal is to make the system more reliable so the fear reduces. Reliability comes from small repeated actions that keep chaos from growing. It also comes from honesty about what "later" really means. If you have saved something for months and never looked at it, the "just in case" has already failed. It has become a weight, not a resource.

The forward test is therefore practical. When you open your camera roll or downloads folder, do you feel you are looking at a tool or at a drawer you would rather not open, and what would change if you treated one small slice of that drawer each week as incoming that must receive a fate rather than as clutter that you vaguely hope will sort itself out?

Creating a donate and discard lane

In 1949 in Chicago, the economist Milton Friedman and his wife Rose began to popularise a deceptively simple idea that later economists would formalise more rigorously: making a choice has an opportunity cost. Keeping one thing often means not keeping another, even when the trade-off is invisible (Friedman, 1962). The concept belongs to markets, but its domestic version is painfully tangible. Every object kept consumes space, attention, and future decision-making. When you keep items without an exit route, you do not merely store them. You agree, implicitly, to keep renegotiating them.

Stuff does not leave by itself.

That is why decluttering so often becomes dramatic. People wait until the home feels intolerable, then attempt a purge: a long weekend of bags and bins and regret, followed by exhaustion and a vow to "never let it get like this again". The vow rarely holds, not because people are weak, but because the system that produced the clutter has not changed. New items continue to enter. Objects continue to drift towards key surfaces. Decisions continue to be postponed. Without a continuous exit route, the home behaves like a bath with the plug in: water can only rise. You can scoop it out occasionally, but the pressure returns.

A donate and discard lane is a plughole.

It is an ongoing, designated place for items leaving the home, kept simple enough that it is used without debate. The lane can be a bag by the door, a box in a cupboard, a corner of the hallway, a shelf in a utility space. The exact form is less important than the function: it converts "this should go" from a vague intention into a physical action. It turns a decision into a state change. State changes are what reduce attention leakage. Without a lane, people keep holding the same decision in their head: I should donate this, I should recycle this, I should get rid of that. The decision never becomes real. The item stays. The mind keeps noticing. The loop remains open.

A scene shows why the lane matters even for households that do not consider themselves cluttered. Someone notices a shirt they no longer wear. They put it aside on a chair, intending to donate it. The chair becomes a staging area. Days pass. The shirt is moved to a different pile. It gets mixed with laundry. It returns to the wardrobe because someone needs the chair. The decision has been made, but the home has no pathway for the decision to exit. The object drifts back into circulation. This is not carelessness. It is systems failure. A lane turns "aside" into "out". The implication is that decluttering is not primarily an act of sorting; it is an act of *removal* made easy.

The hardest part of removal is rarely deciding what to let go of. It is completing the final steps: bagging, storing temporarily, transporting, arranging pick-up, remembering to drop off. These steps are small but sticky, and they are exactly the kind of "tiny tasks" that balloon when they lack a container. A lane provides that container. It reduces the number of steps required at the moment you decide. Instead of deciding and then also solving the logistics immediately, you decide and place the item in the lane. That is a completed action. The logistics can be handled later as a batch, because the items are already gathered. Batching is not about efficiency as a buzzword. It is about reducing context switching. When the lane exists, you stop making a separate plan for each item and start treating outflow as a routine.

This aligns with a broader principle in behavioural science about defaults and friction. Behaviour is shaped less by intention than by what is easy. Richard Thaler and Cass Sunstein popularised the concept of choice architecture: how the design of environments nudges decisions (Thaler and Sunstein, 2008). A donate and discard lane is a piece of domestic choice architecture. It makes the "out" decision easier to execute than the "keep for later" drift. It reduces friction at the exact point where people usually stall. The implication is practical: when "out" is easy, decluttering becomes continuous. When "out" is difficult, decluttering becomes episodic and dramatic.

A second checkable example helps anchor why flow matters. The Frankfurt Kitchen, designed in 1926 by Margarete Schuette-Lihotzky, was built to reduce unnecessary movement and streamline repetitive domestic tasks (Schuette-Lihotzky, 1926). Whether one likes its aesthetics is irrelevant. Its logic is the relevant part: reduce wasted steps by placing tools and pathways where work happens. A donate lane applies the same logic to objects. It is a path. Without a path, you repeatedly move items around the house in a kind of domestic shuffling. Shuffling looks like action. It is often just postponement.

The lane also changes the emotional tone of decluttering. When people attempt a dramatic purge, they often make decisions under fatigue. Fatigue produces regret. Regret makes people hesitant next time. A continuous lane allows decisions to be made in small moments, with less pressure and less exhaustion. The person can remove one item without turning it into an event. This matters because many people do not need a minimalist overhaul; they need a system that prevents drift. Drift is the real enemy. Drift is how unused objects become clutter. Drift is how surfaces become piles. Drift is how the home becomes a space that asks too many questions.

The lane also protects against the false comfort of "donate later". "Donate later" is often a polite way of keeping items indefinitely. People keep a pile of donation items in a spare room or cupboard for months, and the pile becomes a new form of clutter, now accompanied by guilt. The lane avoids this by being designed for movement, not storage. It sits near the exit. It is visible enough to prompt action. It is contained enough not to become a second mess. The behavioural metric is again obvious. Does the pile leave the house regularly, or does it simply migrate from one corner to another?

There is a social dimension too. In shared homes, one person's "keep" is another person's "clutter", and decisions can become contentious. A lane provides a neutral staging point that reduces immediate conflict. It allows the household to agree, implicitly or explicitly, that items placed in the lane are in the process of leaving, not up for repeated debate. It also makes the system fairer. Without a lane, the person who cares most about order ends up doing the labour of decluttering repeatedly. With a lane, participation can become more distributed: anyone can place an item into the lane when they notice it no longer belongs. The system becomes less dependent on one person's vigilance.

A credible limitation needs to be acknowledged. Some people avoid discarding because of genuine scarcity concerns, uncertainty about future needs, or emotional attachments.

Others have limited access to donation points or disposal services. The lane is not a moral prescription to throw things away. It is a structural tool to make chosen outflow easier. The reconciliation is that the lane can include multiple fates: donate, recycle, discard, return, or "to decide" if needed. The key is that the item is removed from key surfaces and out of daily circulation while the decision is made deliberately rather than repeatedly. Even when an item cannot be immediately donated or discarded, placing it in the lane can reduce daily friction and the constant mental ping of seeing it.

Another limitation is that the lane can become a dumping ground if it is not bounded. A bag by the door can become a mountain if nobody ever takes it out. This is a systems problem, not a character problem. The lane needs a cadence, even a light one, for leaving the home. That cadence can be tied to existing routines: errands, school runs, walks, deliveries. The specific timing is less important than the existence of a rhythm. Without a rhythm, the lane fills and becomes a new source of stress. With a rhythm, the lane becomes what it is meant to be: a valve.

The motif that holds this subchapter together is the one bag by the door. It is not symbolic. It is practical. The bag represents an exit route that is always available. It makes decluttering continuous because it reduces the activation energy required to begin. When you can put something into the bag in five seconds, you are more likely to do it. When you have to plan a donation trip before you can even start, you will postpone, and postponement is how clutter wins.

The forward test is therefore not about taste. It is about flow. Where, in your home, do "leaving items" currently live as a vague intention rather than a physical pathway, and what would change if you gave them a lane so that decisions could turn into exits before they turn back into piles?

Chapter 12
Keeping the reset sustainable

A person misses a Sunday. They do not mean to. The week has teeth: travel, illness, family demands, a deadline that spills into the weekend, a day that simply collapses under fatigue. Monday arrives anyway. By Wednesday they feel the familiar drag of open loops and scattered plans, and by Saturday the idea of doing a reset feels heavier than ever, because now it is not only a reset. It is a catch-up. Catch-up is a punishing word. It suggests you are behind in a race you did not agree to run.

Another person keeps the ritual for a while and then overbuilds it. They add steps, refine tools, chase the perfect method. The hour expands. It starts to feel like homework. The ritual becomes a performance, and performance is fragile. When the week gets messy, the person skips the reset because it feels too big to do imperfectly. The system collapses not because the idea was wrong, but because it was made too precious.

The week will change.

That is the central tension of sustainability. The Sunday reset is meant to be a tool, not a test. If it only works in tidy seasons, it does not work. If it demands intensity, it will be abandoned. If it becomes an identity project, it will either inflate into a second job or fail at the first serious interruption. A sustainable ritual is one you can return to when life is noisy, imperfect, and unpredictable. That means it must adapt without losing its structure. It must shrink without disappearing. It must include a re-entry path that does not involve self-punishment.

The stakes are not just about keeping a habit. They are about protecting the very benefit the reset provides: reduced background stress. Background stress returns quickly when open loops multiply and the calendar becomes untrustworthy.

A missed week is not a moral failure, but it is a real shift in conditions. The mind resumes monitoring. The inboxes refill. The waiting-for items become hazy. The house and devices gather friction. If the reset cannot be restarted gently, people drift into a familiar pattern: living in reaction until the pain becomes large enough to trigger an unsustainable overhaul. Sustainability is the avoidance of that boom-and-bust cycle.

A durable ritual is built on a principle that sounds almost too modest to matter: consistency beats intensity. Intensity feels impressive. It also fails easily. Consistency is less flattering and far more effective because it builds trust. Trust, in this book's sense, is the mind's confidence that there is a reliable place and time where open loops will be captured, reviewed, decided, and prepared. That confidence quietens the ping. If the ritual disappears whenever life becomes difficult, the mind stops trusting it, and the ping returns. A small, consistent ritual is therefore not a compromise. It is the point.

The motif for this chapter is the elastic band. An elastic band holds because it stretches. If it cannot stretch, it snaps. A reset hour that cannot stretch downwards, shrinking in busy seasons, snapping back when things are calmer, is not elastic. It is brittle. Brittle rituals force all-or-nothing thinking: either the perfect reset happens, or nothing happens. All-or-nothing thinking is seductive because it simplifies decisions. It is also corrosive because it turns ordinary interruptions into reasons to give up. Elastic rituals treat interruptions as normal and build in a return path.

A return path matters because missed weeks are inevitable. People will travel. People will be ill. Families will need extra attention. Work will spike. If the ritual is designed as a strict streak, missed weeks become shame, and shame is a powerful reason to avoid restarting. A gentle re-entry approach treats missed weeks as data, not as failure. It looks at what has accumulated and responds with a small sequence that restores clarity quickly, even if it cannot restore perfection.

That is the tool mindset: focus on the actions that reduce monitoring and make the week runnable again.

Sustainability also depends on personal ritual cues, not as self-help decoration but as behavioural infrastructure. A repeated time and place help, but so do boundaries that protect the reset from expanding and from being swallowed by other people's needs. A ritual that begins and ends cleanly is easier to honour because it does not feel like a trap. This is where the book's earlier emphasis on endings returns. The reset must teach your mind that organising has a boundary and that the boundary will be respected. When the mind trusts the boundary, it stops resisting the ritual. When the mind fears that the reset will expand endlessly, it will find reasons to skip.

The arc here moves from adapting the hour to different seasons without losing the structure, to re-entering after missed weeks without punishment, to shaping the ritual so it feels calm and repeatable rather than performative. The emphasis remains consistent with everything that came before: less attention leakage, more reliable decisions, fewer avoidable scrambles. Sustainability is not an extra feature. It is the mechanism by which the reset becomes part of life rather than another project.

The unresolved friction that pulls us into the practical work is the one that decides whether this remains a tool or becomes a test. When life gets messy, do you shrink the reset and keep it alive, or do you abandon it because it cannot be done perfectly?

Adapting the hour to seasons

In 1906 in Cambridge, England, William James published *The Principles of Psychology*, arguing that habit is the enormous flywheel of society: it holds us steady not through heroic bursts of will, but through repeated patterns that reduce the need for constant decision-making (James, 1890). The argument has a quiet edge. When life becomes demanding, you do not rise to your ideals. You fall to your habits. The practical question is therefore not whether your Sunday reset is impressive in a calm month. It is whether it survives the weeks when you are tired, travelling, unwell, or needed elsewhere.

Seasons will disrupt you.

A sustainable reset treats disruption as normal rather than as failure. Most people build routines as if life were stable: the same energy, the same availability, the same level of control over weekends. Then a busy season arrives and the routine collapses. The collapse feels personal because the person interprets it as lack of discipline, and that interpretation often triggers an all-or-nothing response: if the full reset cannot happen, nothing happens. Nothing is the worst possible outcome for a system designed to reduce attention leakage, because attention leakage increases precisely when life is chaotic. The moment you most need a small stabilising practice is the moment your standards make it feel impossible.

The central tension is between structure and scope. Structure is the sequence that keeps the hour contained: capture, review, decide, prepare. Scope is how much you try to include within that structure. In calm seasons, scope can expand. In hard seasons, scope must contract. The mistake is to shrink the structure. When the structure is lost, the session dissolves into busywork or avoidance. The wise move is to keep the structure and shrink the scope, so the mind retains the signal that there is still a reliable place where open loops are gathered and commitments are made explicit. The implication is direct: the reset remains trustworthy because it remains recognisable, even when it is smaller.

Trust is the real currency here. The brain relaxes when it trusts a container. It stops monitoring when it believes that certain concerns will be handled at a predictable time. This is why consistency beats intensity. Intensity can produce a dramatic sense of control in a calm week, but intensity is fragile. It disappears under stress, and when it disappears, the mind learns that the system cannot be relied upon. Consistency, even in reduced form, teaches the opposite lesson: the container still exists. That lesson has behavioural consequences. People who keep the ritual in a smaller form tend to check less compulsively during the week, because the system still feels alive.

A simple scene shows how structure can survive a hard season. Someone is travelling or sick or caring for someone else. Sunday arrives with limited time and limited attention. The person who believes the reset must be done "properly" skips it entirely because it cannot be done to standard. They start the week with a mind full of open loops and a calendar that feels less trustworthy. The person who keeps the structure but shrinks the scope does something different. They gather the scattered inputs into one inbox, glance at the week just lived to catch obvious slips, choose a small number of priorities for the week ahead, and ensure the calendar reflects the immovable commitments. The session may be brief. It still produces state changes. The implication is that reduced scope does not mean reduced value. In chaotic weeks, the value of basic containment is unusually high.

Psychology offers language for why all-or-nothing thinking is so corrosive to habit. Perfectionistic standards can create avoidance because any imperfect attempt feels like failure, and failure feels threatening. Research on perfectionism has distinguished between high standards and the harsher tendency to equate imperfection with personal inadequacy (Frost et al., 1990; Hewitt and Flett, 1991). The reset becomes unsustainable when it is treated as a measure of worth rather than as a tool. A sustainable reset treats "small and done" as success in hard seasons. That mindset is not motivational fluff. It is a design choice that keeps the ritual alive.

A named, checkable example from outside personal life helps because it shows that adaptation is a standard feature of robust systems. In aviation, procedures include normal checklists and emergency checklists. The emergency checklist is not longer. It is shorter and more focused, because in stress conditions humans cannot handle increased complexity reliably. The system adapts by shrinking scope while keeping a recognisable structure. The point is not to dramatise your Sunday. It is to borrow the principle: when conditions are harsh, reduce the number of moving parts. Keep the sequence. Protect the essentials.

To adapt the reset to seasons, it helps to define what "essentials" actually are in this context. Essentials are the elements that prevent avoidable surprise and reduce attention leakage: a single capture place that holds new inputs, a calendar that reflects hard commitments, a shortlist of priorities that prevents the week becoming pure reaction, and a clear place to park what cannot be handled now. In a calm season, you might also reset the home basics, triage the inbox, update recurring reminders, and declutter. In a busy season, you might not. The structure remains. The scope shrinks. The aim remains the same: stop the drip.

This is where the motif of the elastic band becomes useful. An elastic band holds because it stretches without snapping. If you pull it too hard, it breaks. A ritual that cannot stretch downwards breaks. It becomes brittle. People then either abandon it or attempt to restart it with a burst of intensity that again cannot be sustained. Stretching downwards is not failure. It is the feature that keeps the ritual from breaking. When life returns to a calmer pace, the band can shorten again. The system recovers because it never fully collapsed.

Adaptation also protects dignity. When someone is ill or in a family crisis, demanding a full reset can be an act of self-cruelty disguised as discipline. The reset is meant to reduce stress, not add a new layer of self-judgement. A reduced reset in such seasons is an act of practical compassion: it respects that cognitive resources are limited and that the week still needs basic structure. It also respects that some open loops cannot be closed in such times. Parking becomes more important. Saying "not now" becomes a form of honesty rather than procrastination. The system remains aligned with reality.

There is, however, a limitation that must be faced: not every season allows even a reduced reset at the usual time. Travel disrupts routines. Care demands can erase weekends. Emergencies can consume attention. The reconciliation is to decouple the ritual from a specific clock time and attach it to a stable trigger where possible: the first quiet hour you can find, the evening before returning to work, the moment after settling into a new location. The ritual's power comes from repetition and recognisable structure, not from perfect timing. A reset done on Monday morning in a travel week may be more useful than a skipped Sunday reset. The point is not to protect the name "Sunday". The point is to protect the container.

A second limitation is that some people use "busy season" as a permanent identity. Everything becomes a busy season. In such lives, scope might always need to be small, and the full version of the reset may never occur. This is not a failure of the method. It is a reality that makes the principle even more important: keep the structure, keep it brief, keep it repeatable. An always-busy life cannot support elaborate rituals. It still benefits from a small, consistent one that prevents constant emergency mode.

The final reason adaptation matters is that it prevents relapse into constant monitoring. When the reset collapses, the mind compensates by keeping more in working memory, checking more often, and treating every incoming message as potentially urgent. The week then becomes noisy, and noise makes it harder to restart the ritual because the ritual now feels like an overwhelming catch-up. A reduced reset interrupts that spiral. It keeps the system from becoming so messy that restarting feels punitive.

The forward test is therefore not whether you can maintain the full hour every week. The question is more revealing. When life becomes difficult, do you shrink the scope while keeping the structure, or do you let the structure collapse because it cannot be done perfectly?

Recovering after missed weeks

In 1962 in Cambridge, Massachusetts, the historian Thomas S. Kuhn published *The Structure of Scientific Revolutions*, describing how people do not change their frameworks smoothly, but through periods of strain, disruption, and then a new normal that looks obvious in hindsight (Kuhn, 1962). The book is about science, not Sunday afternoons, yet its psychological insight transfers. When a system breaks, the hardest part is not the break. It is the moment after, when you must decide whether the break proves the system was never real, or whether it was simply a rupture you can repair.

Missing a week is not betrayal.

It happens for reasons that are usually banal and sometimes painful: illness, travel, deadlines, caring responsibilities, exhaustion, or simply a weekend that collapsed. The problem begins when the missed week is interpreted as a verdict. People tell themselves they have "fallen off", as if the reset were a diet or a streak. That framing turns re-entry into a test of character, and tests invite shame. Shame invites avoidance. Avoidance allows open loops to multiply. Multiplication makes the reset feel even heavier. The cycle is cruel and unnecessary.

The central claim of this subchapter is that recovery must be designed. If recovery is left to willpower, it will be postponed, because the backlog will look intimidating and the mind will anticipate effort without closure. Recovery becomes possible when the reset is treated as a tool, and tools are used in proportion to the job. A missed week does not require a grand punishment session. It requires a re-entry that restores basic containment quickly: capture what has accumulated, pick a small set of priorities, and move forward with a calendar that is trustworthy enough to stop the mind patrolling. This is why "double reset" does not mean double work. It means a slightly different emphasis: stabilise the present before you try to perfect anything.

A scene makes the trap obvious. A person misses two Sundays and sits down on the third with dread. They open their inbox and feel the weight of unread messages. They look at their task list and see items they have been carrying for weeks, now joined by new ones. They feel a pulse of panic and decide they must "get on top of it". They begin scrolling, replying, filing, rewriting, trying to clear everything. The session expands. They become tired. They stop with a sense of failure, because the backlog was always too large to be cleared in one sitting. Now they have taught themselves a lesson: the reset is exhausting and humiliating. They are less likely to return next week. The concept here is punitive recovery. The implication is that shame-based re-entry damages the very habit it is trying to revive.

A gentler re-entry does not avoid reality. It changes the order of operations. It acknowledges that the backlog cannot be erased quickly and that attempting to erase it is the wrong goal. The goal is to restore a reliable container for the week. Reliability reduces monitoring. Monitoring is what makes people feel overwhelmed. A re-entry reset that restores reliability can be brief and still powerful, because it answers the brain's urgent questions: what am I missing, what is due, what matters most now, and what happens next. When those questions are answered, the mind stops generating constant pings, and the backlog becomes a queue rather than a fog.

This is where all-or-nothing thinking needs to be named as a practical error, not a moral flaw. Perfectionistic patterns often treat imperfect action as failure, which leads to avoidance and then to larger backlogs that feel even harder to face. Research on perfectionism has distinguished between high standards and the more punishing tendency to equate mistakes with personal inadequacy (Frost et al., 1990; Hewitt and Flett, 1991). A missed reset becomes, for some people, evidence that they are "not consistent", which then becomes an excuse to abandon the ritual entirely. The correction is to redefine success. Success after missed weeks is not a perfect hour. Success is a restored system: one inbox for inputs, a calendar that reflects reality, and a shortlist that prevents the week becoming pure reaction.

The psychological mechanism that makes a gentle re-entry work is the same one that makes the reset work in general: open loops demand attention until they have a stable fate. Research suggests that unfulfilled goals can generate intrusive thoughts and that forming plans can reduce those intrusions (Masicampo and Baumeister, 2011). After missed weeks, the number of open loops is larger, so the mind's monitoring increases. A re-entry reset reduces monitoring not by completing everything, but by assigning fates: this is due, this is waiting, this is parked, this is deleted, this is scheduled, this is delegated. Each fate is a state change. State changes are calming. They turn the backlog from a threatening mass into a set of defined items, some of which can wait safely.

A named, checkable example from outside personal planning shows why recovery is treated as routine in robust systems. In aviation, procedures include recovery steps after deviations: you do not abandon flight rules because you drifted off course. You correct, reorient, and continue. The language is technical, not moral. Nobody calls a pilot a failure for needing to correct. The system assumes correction will be necessary because reality is dynamic. The personal implication is straightforward. A missed reset is a deviation, not a character judgement. The next step is correction: reorient the system so the week can proceed with less stress.

A double reset, properly understood, is a refusal to replay the missed weeks as a court case. It does not demand that you "make up for" the past. It demands that you regain clarity about the present. It starts with capture because capture reduces the most immediate cognitive load: the fear of forgetting. It then moves quickly to priorities because priorities prevent the week from being consumed by the loudest backlog items. It then moves forward because dwelling is expensive. Dwelling uses attention without changing the world. The reset's value lies in changed states: a message sent, a decision recorded, a time blocked, a project parked, a follow-up noted. Those changes are what turn the system back on.

The motif for this subchapter is the restart button. A restart is not a scolding. It is a function. Devices are designed to restart because processes jam. Life is no different. After missed weeks, the system jams: too many inputs, too little processing, too many unknowns. The temptation is to keep forcing the jammed system, checking constantly, feeling behind, trying to remember everything. A restart is the calmer move. It clears the immediate noise and restores basic functioning. It does not guarantee perfection. It returns you to a state where you can act.

There is a limitation worth admitting, because not every missed-week period is benign. Some missed weeks are caused by genuine crisis, grief, or sustained illness, and the cognitive and emotional capacity available for recovery may be minimal. In such cases, even a gentle re-entry can feel heavy. The reconciliation is to shrink the scope further while keeping the structure intact, as the previous subchapter argued. The re-entry is not a performance. It is a minimal stabilising act. It is allowed to be small. It is allowed to focus only on what is most urgent and most relieving. The system is serving the season, not the other way round.

The forward test is therefore both practical and honest. When you have missed a week or two, do you treat the reset as a courtroom where you must defend your inconsistency, or as a restart button you can press without shame, so the present week can be made clear enough to move on?

Making it your weekly ritual

In 1890 in Cambridge, Massachusetts, William James published *The Principles of Psychology* and described habit as a kind of invisible architecture: patterns that carry us through life with less friction because they reduce the need for constant choice (James, 1890). His point was not romantic. It was pragmatic. When a behaviour must recur, it cannot rely on repeated bursts of self-control. It must be made easier than its alternatives. It must have cues that prompt it and boundaries that contain it. Otherwise it becomes negotiable, and negotiable rituals get eaten by busy weeks.

Ritual is design, not mood.

That is the premise of making the Sunday reset stick. A ritual is not a solemn ceremony. It is a repeated practice that signals to the mind, week after week, that a certain kind of work will happen and that it will end. The mind likes this. It relaxes when it can predict both the start and the finish. Without a ritual, the reset becomes a task you have to decide to do each week. Decision is expensive. Decision invites bargaining. Bargaining invites delay. Delay invites the familiar background stress of open loops. A ritual removes the bargaining by making the reset less of a weekly debate and more of a default movement in the week's rhythm.

The central tension is between usefulness and performance. As soon as someone takes organisation seriously, there is a temptation to turn it into a project: the perfect tools, the perfect routine, the perfect ambience, the kind of ritual that looks impressive and feels fragile. Fragility is the enemy. A ritual that depends on ideal conditions will disappear when conditions are not ideal, which is often. The Sunday reset cannot become another stage for self-evaluation. It exists to reduce attention leakage, not to prove that you are the sort of person who has it all together. When the ritual becomes a performance, it starts to demand attention rather than returning attention. That is a betrayal of purpose.

A small scene shows how performance creeps in. Someone prepares for the reset as if they are preparing for a photo shoot: the desk cleared, the stationery chosen, the playlist curated, the apps organised, the tabs arranged. They begin with a sense of seriousness that is also strangely brittle. Any interruption now feels like contamination. They become irritated if the hour is not pristine. They start optimising the ritual rather than using it. The result is predictable: the ritual feels heavy, so it gets postponed, and once postponed it becomes easier to skip entirely. The concept here is ritual inflation. The implication is that rituals survive by being ordinary.

The structure of the reset has already been established: capture, review, decide, prepare. The question now is how to make returning to that structure feel automatic and safe. This is where cues, rewards, and boundaries matter, not as gimmicks, but as behavioural scaffolding. A cue is the signal that tells the brain, "It is time." A reward is the small closure that tells the brain, "That was worth doing." A boundary is the limit that tells the brain, "This will not take over your life." Together, they reduce the psychological cost of starting and increase the likelihood of repeating.

Cues are not always obvious, and they do not have to be dramatic. In behavioural science, cues are simply triggers that precede a routine. In Charles Duhigg's popular framing, a habit loop includes a cue, a routine, and a reward (Duhigg, 2012). One can argue with the simplicity of the model, yet its usefulness is plain: repeated behaviours are often anchored by repeated prompts. The Sunday reset needs a cue that is stable enough to survive mood changes. That cue might be a time, a place, a particular drink, a certain song, the act of putting on headphones, or the first opening of the calendar. The cue is not superstition. It is a way of making the start less negotiable. When the cue appears, the body knows what to do next.

The reward is equally practical. It is not a gold star. It is the felt experience of closure: the relief of a cleared capture inbox, the calm of a calendar that looks runnable, the satisfaction of a short priority list that makes sense. Rewards do not need to be external. They can be internal, as long as they are noticed. Many people miss the reward because they move immediately from organising into doing, never pausing to register the shift in mental load. The mind learns through experience. If the reset consistently ends in a sense of being trapped in endless work, the mind will resist it. If it ends in a clean stop and a noticeable reduction in noise, the mind will seek it. Ending is therefore part of the reward. It is the moment that teaches the nervous system that organisation is finite.

Boundaries protect the ritual from two threats: expansion and intrusion. Expansion is when the hour becomes a vague block that can grow into the afternoon, turning the reset into a source of resentment. Intrusion is when the reset is repeatedly interrupted by other demands because it has not been claimed as a real commitment. Both threats destroy consistency. A boundary is therefore not merely a time limit; it is a definition of what belongs inside the hour and what does not. When a complex project appears, it goes to parking. When a deep emotional issue appears, it is named and given a next step, not unpacked endlessly. When the urge to rewrite lists appears, it is recognised as cosmetic maintenance and redirected towards decisions and scheduling. Boundaries keep the ritual honest.

A named, checkable example from outside personal life shows why rituals survive when they are designed for ordinary conditions. The UK Government Digital Service's work on GOV.UK, launched in October 2012, was built around user needs and repeatability, not around building an ornate structure that only experts could navigate. The principle transfers. A system that only works when you have abundant time and perfect concentration is not a system; it is a hobby. A ritual that only works in calm weeks is not a ritual; it is a mood. The Sunday reset must be usable in ordinary conditions: some noise, some fatigue, some interruptions, some weeks that are messy. A ritual that assumes mess is more robust than a ritual that assumes perfection.

There is also a deeper human reason to personalise the ritual. People differ. Some settle with silence, others with music. Some think with pen and paper, others with a screen. Some need a visible timer, others need a softer boundary like a fixed ending cue. The ritual should fit the person and the household, not fight them. Personalisation is not indulgence. It is engineering. A ritual that fits is repeated. A ritual that does not fit is resisted. Resistance is expensive because it consumes attention before the hour even begins.

Still, a limitation deserves acknowledgement. Ritual design can become another performance project. People can spend weeks tinkering with cues, tools, and aesthetics as a substitute for doing the reset itself. The ritual becomes a meta-task, a way of procrastinating while feeling productive. The reconciliation is to remember the purpose. The purpose is a calmer, more controllable week. If personalisation increases friction, it has failed. If it decreases friction, it is working. The test is behavioural: do you begin more easily, finish more cleanly, and check less compulsively during the week?

The final motif is the doorway, returning from earlier chapters. A ritual is a doorway you can walk through without arguing with yourself. The doorway has a handle that feels familiar. It opens to a room with a clear shape. It closes behind you when you are done. This is what protects the reset from becoming another open loop. It is also what makes it sustainable across seasons. When life gets hard, you can still walk through the doorway, even if you stay for a shorter time. The ritual remains alive.

The forward test is therefore not whether the reset looks elegant on paper. It is whether you can picture yourself doing it on an unremarkable Sunday when you are tired and the house is noisy, and still beginning anyway because the cue is clear, the boundaries are trusted, and the reward is real.

About the Author

Priya Dhanvel writes about practical ways to reduce everyday friction and make routines feel humane. Her work centres on a simple belief: most people do not need more willpower, apps, or elaborate systems - they need a few reliable rituals that lower the "thinking tax" of modern life. She is especially interested in the invisible workload behind a functioning week: the follow-ups, decisions, and small acts of preparation that rarely get credit but shape how calm or chaotic everything feels.

Across different seasons of life, Priya has seen how easily admin expands to fill every gap, and how quickly background stress disappears when loose ends are given a trusted home. She favours approaches that are light on rules and heavy on repeatability, helping readers build structures that survive busy weeks rather than collapse the moment things get complicated.

A quiet thread in her perspective comes from the long tradition of weekly rest days and resets across cultures - the idea that one day holds space for reflection, preparation, and return. In many households, Sundays have carried this dual role: slowing down while also setting up the week to come. Priya brings that spirit into modern schedules, offering a one-hour practice that respects real constraints and supports a steadier sense of control.

www.ingramcontent.com/pod-product-compliance
Lightning Source LLC
Chambersburg PA
CBHW031342230926
51848CB00002B/349